Saving the Planet

SAVING THE PLANET

---

*The American Response to the
Environment in the Twentieth Century*

Hal K. Rothman

The American Ways Series

IVAN R. DEE   *Chicago*

Library of Congress Cataloging-in-Publication Data:
Rothman, Hal K.
    Saving the planet : the American response to the environment in the twentieth century / Hal K. Rothman.
        p.   cm. — (The American ways series)
    Includes bibliographical references and index.
    ISBN 1-56663-288-9 (cloth : alk. paper) — ISBN 1-56663-301-X (paper : alk. paper)
        1. Environmentalism—United States—Public opinion—History—20th century.   2. Conservation of natural resources—United States—Public opinion—History—20th century.   3. Public opinion—United States.   I. Title.   II. Series.
GE197.R69   2000
333.7'2'09730904—dc21   99-049372

To Lauralee, Talia, and Brent

Contents

Introduction: The Twentieth Century and
Its Many Visions   3
From conservation to environmentalism—continuities and
contradictions.

1 Setting the Stage: The Diverse Currents of
the 1890s   11
Industrialization and reform. John Muir, the Sierra Club, and the
preservation of nature. Federal legislation.

2 Progressive Conservation   34
Theodore Roosevelt and the new approach to conservation.
Addressing water pollution. Gifford Pinchot and scientific forestry.
Implementing Progressive conservation. The Hetch-Hetchy
controversy.

3 Conservation as Business and Labor Policy   60
Jazz Age values. Water in the West. New Deal projects. Effects of
the Great Depression.

4 The Democratization of Conservation   85
Post–World War II social changes. The problems of growth.
Conservation revived. The Echo Park Dam battle.

5 The Rise of Aesthetic Environmentalism   108
The mood of the 1960s. Calls to action. Perils of atomic testing.
Rachel Carson's *Silent Spring*. Paul Ehrlich's *The Population Bomb*.
Environmentalism as a new center of consensus. The Santa Barbara
oil spill.

6 The Limits of Quality of Life   131
The dangerous bargain between industry and its workers. A legal
revolution. The federal response to environmental concerns.
Environmental Impact Statements. The Alaska Pipeline. Earth Day.
Toxic wastes.

7 Backlash: Full Stomachs and Empty Pockets   158
Impact of the oil crisis and the Vietnam War. The Sagebrush
Rebellion. James Watt. Swelling ranks of environmental groups.
Reagan administration policies. The Wise Use movement.

8 A New Environmentalism   184
Three Mile Island. Hazardous waste and Love Canal. New
grassroots activism. Dumping in Nevada.

A Note on Sources   206

Index   210

Saving the Planet

Introduction: The Twentieth Century and Its Many Visions

SINCE 1900, American attitudes toward the natural world have changed as greatly as the nature of life in American society. As the pace of life quickened throughout the century, and the American population became increasingly urban and suburban, the close relationship with the physical world that had dominated preindustrial life acquired mythic significance. Americans have become fascinated by the natural world—the "environment," as we have learned to call it—seeing in it the salvation of themselves and their society, a respite from the pressures of modern life, a return to a more primitive, "purer" way of life. American culture, laws, beliefs, and practices reflect these sentiments; they also appear in the way Americans turn to an idealized nature as moral sustenance and sometimes salvation in times of cultural upheaval. American concern with the environment, shaped by economically driven notions of scarcity during the era when its adherents called themselves "conservationists," has been transformed into a quest for aesthetic perfection, good health, and a quality of life now obscured amidst the hubbub of the postindustrial, commuting monolith that so many Americans know.

Driven largely by affluence, the post–World War II revolution in attitudes called "environmentalism" is one of the many changes wrought by the decline of outright faith in technology and increasing suspicion of the pronouncements of authority, sentiments that characterized the last thirty-five years of the century. Conservation began as a way to save the psychic past and the bounty of the present for the collective future; environmentalism became a way to preserve the present for the individual under the guise of protecting the future. In the end, a fusion between these ideals of "quality of life" and sustainable future pointed a way to a new environmental consciousness for the twenty-first century.

This twist has made the twin concepts of conservation and environmentalism a provocative issue in post-1974 America, with considerable grappling over the meaning of the terms. Conservation, once an idea associated with progress and the greatest good for the greatest number over the long run, is regarded by some as having been coopted by a reactionary cadre interested in preserving individual prerogative. Environmentalism, a product of the incredible affluence of the three decades following World War II, found itself under attack in the leaner times that followed 1974. Some have accused conventional environmentalism of being elitist, concerned with decisions that preserve the prerogatives of the few instead of creating opportunity for the many. Environmentalists have acquired considerable political power, though they often lack the consensus to implement it. These paradoxes characterize the evolution of thinking about the environment in twentieth-century America, from an opportunity to prevent scarcity through efficient use of resources to an all-encompassing philosophy that promises a better quality of life—not by the acquisition of material goods but by the preservation of aspects of the world that would otherwise be lost to progress.

In the United States the twentieth century began with tremendous optimism closely linked to the fabulous expansion of the economy, the rapid growth of population, and the seemingly infinite possibilities for industrial and technological advances and profit that shaped the American ethos. Americans looked at their land and saw the fruits of their labor: cities teeming with people; mansions in enclaves and along the coastlines; museums, railroad stations, and the smokestacks that promised prosperity and, to the more hopeful, human improvement. Even to those who did not share in its wealth, the United States had become a formidable nation, one that believed it could solve all the problems that were the legacy of its rapid transformation. It was easy to be boastful, even pompous, when assessing American prospects.

A sense of loss accompanied the beginning of this great change at the turn of the twentieth century, a constellation of ideas and sentiments that historians call "anti-modern." Some Americans, as the inequity of the world they had created struck them with greater force, wondered whether the changes were all good. Some of these people sought political reform, others created a set of laws to protect the weak from the strong. Still more looked at the continent around them and, seeing its bounty linked to the successes of the nation, believed that their prosperity depended on the wise maintenance of the natural resources that made the country great. They sought a way to preserve nature and culture to evoke the past and to provide a blueprint, both moral and economic, for future growth. Typically men and women of wealth and privilege, they fashioned an idea called "conservation," formulated as the precept of the "greatest good for the greatest number over the long run," in the phrase of its leading proponent, Gifford Pinchot.

This idea, of preserving some of the bounty of the land for the future, was revolutionary in its time. Until the 1890s only an occasional voice—Henry David Thoreau, George Perkins Marsh, or Ralph Waldo Emerson—had seen the American land as anything other than a source of unlimited wealth. For most Americans during the first three hundred years of the European experience in the New World, the response to the sight of a tree had been to cut it down and make it useful: into shelter, into transportation, into fuel, into an article for storing food. Descended from the peoples of Europe, the ethnically polyglot Americans came from a land of want: they had been short of land, timber, grasses, game, and other necessities of life. Their reaction to the bounty of North America was entirely reasonable. People of the culture of wood, they saw abundance and prosperity in the many trees of the northeastern states, the tall grasses of the Midwest, the rich loamy soils of the Mississippi Delta. That their behavior dispossessed the native peoples of the continent bothered them only slightly. They had found Eden, a place of plenty, and they set about civilizing it with great earnestness. When conservation appeared on the American scene, its proponents found that breaking the habits of ten generations in the New World came hard.

These first conservationists ran contrary to the basic beliefs of their society. In a world that promoted individual gain even at the expense of the community, they counseled restraint of individual acquisitiveness. Building from a series of traditions in Old World and New World thought, and borrowing liberally from native cultures, they fashioned an ethos of responsibility. In a time when resources still seemed infinite, conservationists pointed to limits. In a moment of unbridled optimism only slightly tinged with undercurrents of discontent, they openly challenged the dominant ideas of their society. In the process they created the basis for an American countertradition that extended throughout the twentieth century. While these middle-class and efficiency-oriented conservationists might have been uncomfortable in the rapidly changed circumstances of the post–World War II world, the ideas they helped develop became environmentalism, an American secular religion.

The conservation movement of the early twentieth century was only a departure point. As an idea it held considerable sway until 1945. In the remarkable period of prosperity that followed World War II and ended only with the combination of Vietnam-era inflation and an oil shortage in 1974, a new set of ideas rose to the fore. They had their roots in the growing sense of entitlement widely felt in American society, and in a rapidly developing sentiment that progress was dangerous, even tainted. They also reflected growing grassroots participation in politics. The basis in efficiency that had marked conservation seemed narrow and mechanistic in a world given to more personal goals and global interpretations, in a world first of incredible optimism and then of retrenchment. While the idea of preserving for the future retained considerable power, the idea of making the moment special for the self became the watchword of the day.

Called environmentalism, this new set of ideas took the precepts of conservation further than ever before. Where conservation promised a better, more prosperous society through efficiency, environmentalism sought improved quality of life for individuals. Instead of merely preserving resources for the future as conservation had done, environmentalism advocated a shift in the way Americans perceived their world. By the 1970s Americans typically understood the concept of limits, even if they did not always adhere to it. Environmentalism often advocated not only restraint but setting aside some of the bounty of prosperity for all time, simply for its positive impact on the quality of everyone's life. Some things could be preserved forever and shared—special lands, animal and fish species—in an effort to assuage not the wallet but the psyche. Where conservation offered restraint to save bounty for the future, environmentalism advocated preservation as a symbolic and psychic salve to the wounds caused by modern society.

The individual and community impulses in environmentalism appear contradictory, but most proponents of environmentalism saw little or no tension between the two. Environmentalists also embraced a certainty that bordered on

the religious. They often believed in a near-utopian perfectibility, achieved through their own efforts. In essence, environmentalists framed the individualist goals of their
message in the context of community goals; it was as if they
said, "Better for me, better for all." This melding of different
interests, and the inconsistencies inherent in them, typified not
only environmentalism but other reform efforts of the time.

The Echo Park Dam controversy at Dinosaur National
Monument in northwest Colorado in the late 1940s and early
1950s, and the publication of Rachel Carson's *Silent Spring*,
sparked the complicated phenomena that became environmentalism. The opposition to the Echo Park Dam occurred
not on traditional conservationist grounds—that it was ineffi-
cient—but on larger questions of the use of open space and the
sanctity of Dinosaur National Monument, reserved in perpetuity by law but now threatened by a dam and reservoir. *Silent
Spring* showed the downside of progress, a world potentially
without songbirds, a threat to the beauty and indeed the
wholeness of the nation. Together these two events provoked
a quality-of-life movement which uncomfortably included
both the preservation of the outdoors and protection from
toxic and hazardous wastes, emissions, and other kinds of pollution.

The new interest in protection from the hazards of industrial society spoke to one of the great objectives of the quality-
of-life movement: to ensure that human endeavor was as
risk-free as possible. Americans had long assumed that prosperity and risk were closely linked, but the generation that
came of age after World War II refused to accept such a notion. As the risks of industrial endeavor piled up and a changing global economy forced Americans to accept significant
risk in the workplace, the dangers of toxics became better
known and more widely feared. The result was an energized
debate that challenged the axiom that risk and reward had to

be part of the same package. In their desire to perfect society, Americans sought the impossible: risk-free industrial and nuclear enterprises. In this attitude they revealed not only a class-based sense of privilege but a clear dimension of the utopianism that accompanied the rise of American environmentalism.

Expanding to such urban themes as pollution, noise, and contamination, environmentalism was also able to extend its reach beyond the middle class. Urban advocates were as likely to be minority and poor as they were to be college-educated and upper-middle-class white, and they saw the world in holistic terms. Where traditional environmentalists tended to see sacred space, places that were so beautiful, spectacular, and uplifting that they could not be defiled, and, on the other hand, profane, ordinary, everyday places, urban environmentalists wondered why *any* part of the world had to become fouled. Using the techniques of civil rights and other protesters, they noisily complained about the unintended consequences of industrial life. As the United States became an overwhelmingly urban nation, the condition of the home became as important as that of faraway sacred space.

After 1974, when the nation entered a period of diminishing prosperity, many Americans became skeptical of an environmentalism that seemed to lock up resources for the pleasure of the few. Yet even these critics wanted their skies clean and their water pure, their parks open and their wildlife protected. As a nation, Americans accepted a loose notion of stewardship, intimately tied to their sense of personal needs. With just a minor twist, 1980s- and 1990s-style environmentalism could easily fit under that heading.

The values of environmentalism thus challenge the notion of progress in a complicated way. They do not suggest that progress is bad; instead they question what constitutes progress and whether that progress is worth its price. In a famous axiom, a noted environmentalist once remarked that the building of six houses on seven vacant lots could not be challenged, but building on the last empty lot was a foolish gesture worthy of opposition. The point was that some, even most, land could be used for human endeavor and comfort without a fight, but all could not. Environmentalism asks questions about what people need and how they should go about attaining their objectives. It tells stories of people committed to both enlightened self-interest and altruism, people of privilege and people of poverty, activists and bureaucrats. These sentiments, and the responses to them, chart the primary path this book will follow.

1

Setting the Stage:
The Diverse Currents of the 1890s

IN 1890 the industrial revolution and its aftermath were changing the very basis of American life. American raw materials increasingly fueled the world economy, American goods were achieving dominance in world markets, and American companies expanded their operations around the globe. John D. Rockefeller's Standard Oil led the way. Standard Oil controlled oil—from the well that brought it to the surface, to the canister in which retail customers purchased it—and domination of that crucial industry conveyed great social power as well as enormous profit.

Cities grew, defying the scale of earlier communities. As agriculture lost ground, rural Americans joined the incredible stream of immigrants who came to American cities in search of a better life. There was no way for political leaders to keep up with such growth, even if they had the ideas and tools to do so. Thirty thousand people called Chicago home in 1850; by 1880 the town had reached 500,000, and the growth continued, more than tripling to 1.7 million just twenty years later. The nation had a new size and scale, a glisten that came from steel and machine oil, a polish, a verve, a swagger. Americans could be proud when they looked at their nation, emerging from adolescence to maturity and parity with European powers.

The downside to growth and change was a sense of loss of what the author John Dos Passos later remembered as "the quiet afterglow of the nineteenth century." Agriculture experienced this loss more severely than any other segment of American society. Believing that ownership of land would bring wealth, most Americans dreamed of attaining independence by working their own plot of land. This sense of freedom had been impossible for most of their forebears in Europe. Especially groups such as African Americans, who experienced freedom as control of their personal as well as their social lives, coveted the freedom and self-determination of the self-employed agriculturalist. Thomas Jefferson's mythic yeoman farmer, the backbone of the ideal American republic, lived on in the hopes and dreams of millions of immigrants, freedmen and women, and everyone else who envisioned the farm as a bastion of American life. Government had encouraged such aspirations with the Homestead Act of 1862, which granted 160 acres of the public domain to anyone who paid a filing fee and improved the land for five years, and with the Morrill Land Grant Act of the same year, which created universities with an agricultural mission. When the transcontinental railroad linked the nation in 1869, thousands went west in the hope that prosperity would accompany their newfound independence.

For most Americans, this equation of land with independence was at best a mixed blessing. At the very moment that large numbers acquired title even to rich loam, land ownership became less important than possession of even a small piece of the production mechanisms of American society. Although well-meaning and skilled individuals chose a future in agriculture, they could not overcome the fundamental redistribution of power and wealth that followed industrialization.

Urban centers with their enormous steel mills, smelters, ship-yards, and machine-tool factories dwarfed agriculture and turned it from the most important sector of the American economy to a producer of raw materials in a world of finished products. For many Americans, especially those who enjoyed privilege in the years before the Civil War, this change dislocated and distressed them, and over time created fissures in American society.

In the cities of the 1890s, even beneficiaries of the transformed American landscape showed signs of discomfort with the consequences of industrialization. Changing perceptions of what constituted a democracy anticipated a more closely regulated social order. In the 1870s Americans embraced the English social theorist Herbert Spencer, who advanced the concept of Social Darwinism and described the inequity that resulted from industrialization as "survival of the fittest." Spencer's assessment of the world Americans inhabited seemed to explain change and to justify the divisions it created in society—the incomparable wealth and the abject poverty that coexisted everywhere anyone looked. By the 1890s the nation no longer blindly accepted such pronouncements. Instead many Americans clearly recognized the flaws of industrialization, its enormous and unevenly distributed toll on society. More important, they no longer passively accepted Spencer's doctrine. A search for other philosophies to guide the American nation began in earnest. Writers and thinkers such as Henry George, author of an 1879 social reform treatise called *Poverty and Progress*, which advocated a tax on the unearned increase in land values to permit all Americans to live in comfort, and Lester Frank Ward, whose 1883 book *Dynamic Sociology* debunked Spencer's theories, challenged the smugness that once permeated industrial America. By the depression of 1893, the most severe economic decline to date, the number of Americans who felt the need for reform nearly matched those who continued to accept the social structure of industrialization.

In the years following the Civil War, Americans had come to regard their continent with new and different eyes. Much of the nineteenth century had been devoted to expanding the nation, beginning with the Louisiana Purchase and the Lewis and Clark expedition of 1803–1805, and before the 1890s those terms had dominated national discussion. Manifest Destiny, the idea that Americans were preordained to control the vast temperate zone of North America, was a widely shared idea. In 1890 the Census revealed that a contiguous line of settlement of no less than two people per square mile now stretched from coast to coast. Drawing upon this information, a young historian from Portage, Wisconsin, Frederick Jackson Turner, proposed what has come to be called the Frontier Thesis. Turner believed that the United States had been special because of its open land, a "safety valve" which could accommodate excess population. This frontier had been the crucible of democracy, Turner insisted, the catalytic factor in creating democratic institutions. It was the seed of what was best about the American nation. Without it, Turner mused, the nation ever after would be different, muted, transformed. Turner's idea struck a chord in American society. Theodore Roosevelt, on his way to becoming the figure who defined the age, wrote the young scholar that he had pulled from the air the great issue of the moment, that he had put his finger directly on the problem of the age.

Pronouncements like Turner's fed a growing sense of discontent in American society. Not only had the world changed very quickly, not only had the scope and scale of life been altered so greatly that even beneficiaries worried about its consequences, but the most basic traits of American society seemed at risk. If as Turner announced, the frontier made Americans unique, large questions followed. Without it, would the nation become another Europe, stratified, torn by strife, and, most essentially, lacking opportunity? Would Americans be able to find ways to prosper without the assurance that there was more—land, water, coal, copper—beyond the horizon? A crisis loomed. American institutions had functioned in one fashion until 1890. It was clear to many that if they did not change, the advantages of American society might dwindle and even disappear, leaving the great democratic experiment quite ordinary.

A broad segment of American society responded with the beginnings of a new ethos. Checks on growth and change were deemed essential. In an industrial society, Americans had to invent new systems for regulating themselves; the combination of social sanction and small-town practices that sufficed before the Civil War proved inadequate as cities grew and people lived anonymously, apart from a clearly defined social structure. A growing segment of the public felt compelled to reinvent the nature of American life. This sentiment gave rise to the idea of reform that came to possess American society as the nation sought to redefine its direction and shape its future in a manner different from its post–Civil War past.

Yet few mechanisms existed in American life that offered ways to initiate change. The ideas that underpinned democracy resulted from a preindustrial mercantile world. The rapid expansion of industry, the wealth it created, and the political power that flowed to it stifled the means of discussion that had fostered communication in American society. In the last quarter of the nineteenth century money dominated, and power and wealth were synonymous. Despite a growing and militant labor sector, the agrarian turmoil that spawned populism, and cities that seemed increasingly dangerous and even sordid, when the middle class felt uncomfortable it could turn only to individuals. Social institutions were devoted to other goals.

Efforts at reform began as discontent rather than action. Ordinary people looked around their world and saw problems; individually they conceived of solutions, and a few even began to implement them. Throughout the 1890s their efforts were diffuse, spread over the national landscape. Loose strands of reform moved through American society like an electrical current. Beginning with the Interstate Commerce Act of 1887 and the Sherman Anti-Trust Act of 1890, a move to regulate business gathered momentum. At the same time reformers followed the lead of Jane Addams in launching the settlement houses that taught women the economic and cultural skills to climb out of poverty. Jacob Riis published *How the Other Half Lives*, a look at life in the New York slums, and it attracted the attention of the middle class. In a changing society, Americans looked for ways to reconstitute order from the vast and chaotic change that was the legacy of industrialization.

Sensing itself disfranchised by the growth of industrial society, the old middle class provided the impetus for this change. These community leaders—clergy, shopkeepers, lawyers, and other professionals—who had guided society before the Civil War no longer served as a social and moral compass for the nation. Cornelius Vanderbilt and Andrew Carnegie, possessors of great fortunes who wore their wealth ostentatiously, replaced community leaders as the defining force in American society. Industrialization fostered a new set of signs and symbols, and the new configuration excluded the old leaders of the decentralized rural nation. As they looked to reassert themselves in national social and cultural life, the once powerful found their position diminished. They coveted the status they had once enjoyed and the prerogative that accompanied it, and sought ways to regain power and position.

The dislocating nature of change also made many Americans yearn for a simpler time. In this most common of human impulses, people of the late nineteenth century sought an idyllic moment in the past from which to begin to rebuild a present they could first comprehend and then tolerate. They wanted to make a world in which they were more comfortable, one that resembled what seemed to be the clearly defined constraints of the pre–Civil War period. In their view, nostalgic but also genuine, the problems of the antebellum world seemed simple and solvable, especially in comparison to the consequences of industrialization. In this effort to reshape the present along the lines of the past, the need for change combined forward- and backward-looking perspectives.

Growing reform sentiments took on many guises. When it encountered business, reform was hard-nosed and pragmatic. The Interstate Commerce Act and the Sherman Anti-Trust Act both addressed economic concerns, though without meaningful enforcement mechanisms. But efforts to solve social problems, to bring morality to bear on the questions of the day, revealed an idealism that approached utopianism as well as much evidence that people saw reform as a way to implement their own prejudices.

If Americans alive in 1860 looked closely at their country in 1890, they scarcely recognized it. Vast cities, teeming neighborhoods filled with people speaking foreign languages, industries belching smoke, railroad lines consuming huge expanses of urban areas, and shipyards of colossal scale seemed to crowd the nation. Animals once common had disappeared or were disappearing; the buffalo, or American bison, had been reduced to a relict population, unable to survive without human intervention, and the passenger pigeons that once filled the skies were poised for extinction. Even Native Americans, once seen as a threat to the nation, were perceived as casualties of expansion, inspiring a well-intended if tragic effort to save them by teaching them cultural practices such as agriculture and domestic work. Huge chunks of forest from Michigan to Minnesota had been cut for timber; the northeastern states seemed almost bare of trees as a result of voracious harvesting. Land had been cultivated, people settled almost everywhere, and the continent, once regarded as wild and infinite, seemed tame and finite, controlled by the power of humanity and the forces of industry and technology.

The United States had fancied itself nature's nation long before the end of the nineteenth century. When Americans began to fashion a national identity, what stood out about their nation was the expansiveness, beauty, and sublime nature of the land they inhabited. The Adirondacks, the White Mountains of New Hampshire, the wilds of Virginia all offered nature as glorious as the grand political experiment of democratic nation-building. The derisive comments of Europeans such as the Comte Georges de Buffon, who in correspondence with Thomas Jefferson mocked what he perceived as the inferior physical nature of the New World, only spurred Americans' pride in their natural treasures as the equivalent of European culture. From James Fenimore Cooper's *Leatherstocking Tales* to Charles F. Lummis's *A Tramp Across the Country* and the work of John Burroughs, from the Hudson River School of painters to the glorious landscapes of Thomas Moran, Americans fashioned an identity that elevated their natural world to a position of preeminence. When Americans looked at nature, they saw a validation of their national experience that they loudly insisted—and secretly hoped—Europe could not match.

The fusing of reform currents and love for America's surroundings occurred in fits and starts throughout the 1890s, but never came to fruition. Like other manifestations of reform, most achievements remained independent of any structured national organization. Individuals thought in the compartmentalized terms of their own concerns. People who favored the protection of forests saw themselves sharing goals and objectives with those who advocated the management of water resources. Supporting the creation of a national park hardly predicted wide involvement in similar causes. Even those who sought to preserve the prehistoric past did not see a commonality of purpose with others who held similar feelings about animals and birds.

John Muir came to embody the urge to preserve, though his personal interest in wild nature far exceeded his passion for the historic or cultural past. Born in Scotland in 1838 and raised on a farm in Wisconsin, Muir was the archetypal first-generation American. His father used the boy's labor as a resource to build the family farm in the manner that typified the age, and in Muir's case capped it off with a dose of Calvinism that made for a dour household. Daniel Muir even forbad John's mother to sing her children the songs of the Scottish Highlands she so loved. It was a hard life of work, without joy or often even laughter. John Muir showed a preternatural talent for mechanical invention and began a successful career in factory management until one day in 1868 when a sliver of a file shot into his eye and blinded him. His other eye went sympathetically blind, and for weeks Muir could not see. During his blindness the young man experienced an epiphany. He suddenly realized that the meaning of life involved the works of God, not the attempts of humanity to shape the universe. When his sight returned in both eyes, he determinedly devoted himself to nature. Walking from Indianapolis to the Gulf of Mexico and boarding a steamer for California, he headed for the wilds of Yosemite, high in the Sierra Nevada Mountains, to revel in, admire, and worship wild nature.

In Yosemite, Muir became the first genuine American advocate of the preservation of nature for its own sake. He developed an ethic of respect for the physical world that took its shape from the religious fundamentalism of his upbringing and replaced reverence for a deity with worship of nature as

God's purest handiwork. Muir lived in a cabin with running water—a river ran through its center—and spent weeks and months in the high elevations of Yosemite, sleeping under the stars and greeting the change in seasons with a delight that seemed to many eccentric if not absurd. He climbed trees in thunderstorms so that he could be closer to his Creator. He lived in the rain and cold without cover, traveled with only the most basic tools and provisions, and generally made himself as close to nature as an individual could. His pronouncements on the beauty of nature and spiritual value spoke loudly in a culture where the costs of change were high. Muir became a celebrity while living in Yosemite and continued on to a career as writer, mountaineer, scientist, and the leading advocate of the preservation of wilderness for its own sake.

In an America increasingly obsessed with nature as a vestige of the nation's greatness, Muir's experiences—and the elegant way he wrote about them—carried deep symbolic meaning. Self-trained, he won respect as a scientist for discovering that glaciers were alive; his folksy approach to science helped mitigate the widespread social tension between folk wisdom and emerging professionalism. He imbued nature with the spirit of the deity in a fashion that the people of the late nineteenth century could welcome. He seemed descended from Natty Bumpo, the latest in a straight line of American literary heroes who took their knowledge directly from the natural world. In the 1880s and 1890s Muir spoke for nature with a clarity and simplicity that few other advocates of any cause displayed. He became an American folk figure, capable of persuading people far different from him of the need to preserve pure, untrammeled nature.

From Muir's work and from the many individuals who shared at least some of his convictions emerged an organization that defined the loose affiliations and often contradictory impulses that became the conservation movement: the Sierra

Club. The prototype for the first generation of conservation organizations and the most powerful voice in early conservation, the Sierra Club was founded in 1892 in California by Muir and other influential Californians. At its founding the club contained both a strong preservationist wing and a powerful group that advocated utilitarian conservation. Sierra Club members came chiefly from the upper classes, people with intact fortunes who could afford to think of nature for its beauty and not for the wealth it might provide. Although Muir's passionate fundamentalism about wilderness preservation derived from a near-religious experience, he was a self-taught man of letters and science who, until he married at the age of forty-two, often teetered on the edge of poverty by choice. Most of the other founders of the Sierra Club not only were affluent, they were educated civic and social leaders as well. Robert Underwood Johnson of the *Century Magazine*, one of the bellwether periodicals of the early twentieth century, played an instrumental role in founding the organization. Stanford University president David Starr Jordan was also a founder, as was attorney Warren Olney, later the reform-oriented mayor of Oakland, California, and the scientist Joseph LeConte, a University of California professor who shaped the teaching of science throughout the state. The early Sierra Club had power, standing, influence, access to wealth, and a worldview that shared the ideas of the time and mirrored its dominant ethos.

This meeting of wealth, power, and education was representative of individuals who were drawn to early conservation as a way to preserve the prerogatives of an orderly past in a disorderly present. Conservationists had their roots in the antebellum middle class, precisely the people who felt that the industrial transformation of the late nineteenth century had lowered their stature in American society. They strongly believed that the past had been better than the present, and that it offered truths that could be used to make a better society. Individually the response of this group was to assert its claims to leadership not in the gauche economic terms of the Gilded Age but in a growing emphasis on the quality of life. In the late 1880s Johnson and Muir sought national park status for Yosemite, then designated as a state park. In their view the attributes of Yosemite were nationally significant. It reflected the powerful beauty of the pristine continent, a value much diminished in the industrial world but resurrected by the growing sense of loss that accompanied industrialization and urbanization. By rescuing Yosemite and placing it before the nation, early conservationists hoped to foster a new way of looking at the late nineteenth-century moment. In this way the Sierra Club foreshadowed progressivism as the diverse strains of reform sentiment began to gather momentum.

The early Sierra Club exuded a built-in arrogance that typified the privileged of the age. Generally its members believed that their way of seeing and understanding the world was best, that they and people like them were the only ones entitled to an opinion on the subject of conservation in the United States, and that others, especially those business leaders who had come to dominate American political life in the late nineteenth century, should defer to their judgment. This set of expectations highlighted the class status of the early Sierra Club. Privilege and power went hand in hand with support for conservation.

To the early Sierra Club, Yosemite was the center of the universe, the place that first defined the organization and where it learned its peculiar brand of politics. Although Yosemite had become a national park in 1890, just before the club was founded, it remained under the jurisdiction of a state commission, a situation that never pleased Muir. The commission did not see Yosemite in Muir's terms. Ranchers with land leases grazed their animals in Tuolomne Meadows in the center of the park, and hog pens in the valley were an eyesore as well as an aromatic reminder that Muir's sense of the area's value did not hold much sway. For years Muir was loathe to challenge the commission's decisions, but the Sierra Club forced his hand. In 1893 charter member Charles D. Robinson, an artist, was so offended by the havoc in Yosemite that he pressured the organization to challenge state control, a prospect that split the membership. Some in the club, such as Warren Olney, believed that transferring the park to the federal government would cost the state prestige and trap the club in a position of opposing the development of California. Others sided with Robinson, seeing in federal management a claim for the unique treatment of the place at a time when the federal government actively managed only a very few places.

This struggle revealed the limitations of the early conservation movement. Many Sierra Club members were also important players in the growth of California. They saw progress and preservation—two seemingly opposed activities—as discrete objectives that did not conflict. Muir and a few of the most outspoken members already perceived that the two positions could not always be easily reconciled. They pushed for a public stance that included advocacy, in many ways anathema to the class of people who made up the Sierra Club. To advocate meant to sully impartial hands in the muck of politics. People of the stature of most Sierra Club members did not lightly break the conventions of their class. As a result, a rift took shape even before the diverse sentiments that supported the idea of managing the present for the future acquired a label.

The split in the Sierra Club also reflected the varied expectations of its members. For some the club was a vehicle for the exercise of power. For others it was merely a social organization of people who enjoyed outdoor activity and who lived in a place where such opportunities abounded. The "High Trip," an annual pack journey to the most remote and inaccessible areas of the Sierra Nevada, embodied this second outlook, the essence of the early club. On the High Trip men and a few women of power and wealth in turn-of-the-century California joined together to brave the wild. It was not a political act by any means but a test of fortitude in an era when people could believe that civilization—"overcivilization" to Muir and others like him—deprived people of the essence of life. Mirroring John Muir, Jack London, and others, Sierra Clubbers sought to commune with a fierce and sometimes frightening nature, and they developed an outspoken pride in their efforts. Although a few women were present in these early gatherings, the predominant tone was male—and aggressively so. The High Trip became the signature event in the life of the club, the defining symbol of its early history. Those who braved the trip could gain admittance to the inner circle. On this level, early conservation mimicked the posturing for status and prestige among men.

With the determined and sometimes fanatical Muir as the lead voice in 1890s conservation, the Sierra Club became an activist organization. Reluctance remained before 1900, but direction was clear. Muir was renowned as a scientist and writer and had the ear of many nationally powerful individuals. The battle to make Yosemite a national park catapulted him into the public eye. Although he was in his fifties, Muir was a tireless worker. Even those who opposed the entrance of the Sierra Club into the public realm often succumbed to the charms of the charismatic and insistent Scotsman, "John of the Mountains," the one man in the United States who seemed closer to nature than to the human species. Although he talked incessantly and could be quite dogmatic, Muir consistently won over his opponents, and conservation followed his lead.

Muir's efforts were not unprecedented. Congress had already passed a number of conservation measures that addressed specific concerns in specific places, and were supported by local representatives. Separately these laws protecting natural and cultural phenomena were barely impressive; together they constituted the legal roots of American conservation.

The first and most important of these acts in the 1890s was Amendment 24 to the General Appropriations Act of 1891, which gave the president authority to establish forest reserves —later renamed national forests—from publicly owned land in order to prevent downstream flooding caused by the denuding of watersheds. Stands of timber greatly slowed runoff, and in the semi-arid states and territories of the West, where rain came in "gullywashers" (great amounts in brief periods), the expansion of commercial timber-cutting often meant the inundation of downstream communities. The threat of flooding was so great that congressmen barely understood the power contained in this simple little clause. The amendment passed with little discussion.

Amendment 24 was a harbinger not only of the idea of conservation but also of the centralizing of power in the presidency. A president now needed no authority from Congress to proclaim a forest reserve, nor did elected officials at lower levels of government have any recourse if they opposed an executive declaration. The bill gave the chief executive unchecked discretion over the fate of public lands, a power not seen as terribly important by those who ran American society at the time. Public lands had already been picked over, and industry was usually interested only in the mineral resources beneath the ground. Yet ceding this power to the president had important consequences and foreshadowed a changing scenario in American politics. It reinvested the presidency with power and moral authority. After the assassination of Abraham Lincoln, a series of weak presidents had diminished the office.

Some, such as Benjamin Harrison of Indiana, proved to be friends of conservation, but most remained indifferent except to the powerful interests that had put them in the White House. As a groundswell rose against the power of industry, it included a search for a place that was immune to the temptations of position and could resist the entreaties of the powerful. The presidency became the de facto location, a position seen as beholden to but somehow exempt from the predatory industrialists of the era.

The practical power of Amendment 24 was limited. The law conferred only the power to designate lands and provided no substantial mechanisms for their administration. Although the appointment of forest supervisors followed the proclamation of forest reserves, these were usually political perquisites dispensed in the manner of other patronage. Forest supervisors who were relatives of political supporters or financial backers were common; some never even left their quarters to view the lands in their charge. Yet despite the lack of serious guardianship, a principle had been established: not only could a sitting president change the status of federally owned land with a signature, but large tracts of land could be set aside for purposes other than individual economic gain. Amendment 24 began a generation of legislation that invested the presidency with unchecked jurisdiction. An important part of it, such as the Forest Reserve Act of 1897 which established a formal system of forest administration, dealt with the protection of nature and its preservation for future use.

Amendment 24 added a new direction to public land policy in the United States. From its founding, the nation had been continually divesting itself of its holdings. The Homestead Act was only the most widely recognized of such legislation. The Timber Culture Act of 1873, the Timber and Stone Act of 1878, and John Wesley Powell's proposed 2,500-acre homesteads were part of an ongoing effort to turn federal land over to individuals who would then become the nation's agricultural and industrial backbone. Amendment 24 had the opposite effect. It withdrew land from private use for a public purpose, a trend that would become even more pronounced as the principles of conservation gained sway in Congress.

During the 1890s the cultural heritage of the nation also drew the attention of Congress. After the great surveys of the 1870s, Americans knew of the West's cultural wonders as well as its natural attractions. The remnants of prehistoric civilizations—among them places known today as Mesa Verde National Park, Chaco Culture National Historic Park, and Canyon de Chelly National Monument—gained the attention of explorers and the settlers who followed them. Observers marveled at the architectural complexity of prehistoric ruins, which revealed people of sophistication who left with scarcely a trace. To an American nation still feeling inferior to Europe, the remnants of a seemingly urban prehistory offered a counter to the still loud and still offensive cry from the Continent that the New World had no real civilization.

The move to save American prehistory began in the wet, cold Northeast, thousands of miles from the dry deserts that preserved so much of prehistoric life in North America. Easterners of wealth and privilege developed interest in the ruins, beginning with the efforts of John Wesley Powell's Bureau of American Ethnology and broadening into support for archaeological excavations organized by such institutions as the American Museum of Natural History in New York and the Peabody Museum at Harvard University. There seemed an urgency to preserving Southwestern prehistory. Not only were Native Americans a vanishing race, archaeological sites were being mauled by tourists and others in search of mummified human remains, baskets, pots, and other relics of prehistoric life. The argument for recognizing this American cultural heritage, coupled with an impending sense of loss generally felt in upper-class America, gave the protection of prehistoric ruins greater social significance.

As early as 1880, Americans wrote to federal agencies and officials to advocate the protection of archaeological ruins, but no organized protection for such places existed. The only federal mechanism was the power to withdraw lands temporarily from the public domain. Permanent protection required congressional action, often a slow and serpentine endeavor. Temporary withdrawal, a process by which land was set aside until its best disposition could be determined, became the tool of choice for federal agencies interested in preserving prehistory on federal land. By the end of the century such designated lands included those rich with archaeological ruins in Colorado, Utah, and the territories of New Mexico and Arizona.

Temporary withdrawal had one basic advantage: it meant that the land could not be claimed by an individual. No program for its use accompanied the designation. Under the best of circumstances, an informative sign was posted on the property. In most cases, temporary withdrawals existed on paper, and they did little to protect the land or its resources. If anything, knowledge of the withdrawal often sent a message to amateur archaeologists and others looking for valuable artifacts.

Into the first decade of the twentieth century, temporary withdrawal was the only available strategy for conservationists. An act of Congress in 1893 established the first permanent reservation, the Casa Grande Ruins Reservation, now Casa Grande National Monument in central Arizona. Then more than four hundred years old, the three-story adobe structure had been old when the Spanish priest Father Junípero Serra wrote of it in the eighteenth century. The sponsors of the legislation—and it seemed all its supporters—came from Massachusetts, where interest in the archaeological past was intense. Yet the bill that established the reservation set no statutory precedent. It merely proclaimed a specific place without offering a system. In the absence of evident economic value, preservation for cultural reasons lagged behind efforts to conserve commercial resources to ensure future supply.

A third type of legislation, wildlife protection, also appeared in this era. Americans had begun to note the impact of their advance on the bird and animal populations of the continent. James Fenimore Cooper's first novel, *The Pioneers*, published in 1824, set the tone for awareness. In it a group of drunken hunters blast away at a sky darkened with pigeons, only to have the dead birds fall into a lake as the hunters laugh and drunkenly wander off. An aristocrat, Judge Marmaduke Temple, the Leatherstocking Natty Bumpo, and Chingachgook, the last of the Mohegan people, look on with dismay and disgust—establishing ever after a line of sympathy that bound these different types. Those who advocated wildlife protection felt close to this odd triumvirate.

With expansion across the continent, once-abundant species were disappearing. The American bison had enjoyed a range that stretched from the Gulf of Mexico and even the Atlantic Ocean to the Rocky Mountains and beyond on the northern plains. Growing numbers of Native American ponies on the Great Plains and westward expansion along the Oregon Trail cut into the buffalo range and diminished their population; hunters working for the railroads in the 1860s decimated the herds. By 1890 so few remained that only human intervention assured their survival. As more and more people poured into the West, searching for infinite bounty, the destruction of animal species by organized and wanton hunting became common. Such actions symbolized a form of destruction that growing numbers of the upper classes—many of whom admired the old values of Cooper—felt was despicable.

One of the most prominent organizations to stand against indiscriminate hunting was the Boone and Crockett Club, founded by the future president Theodore Roosevelt and the noted author and early conservationist George Bird Grinnell. Both men took a jaundiced and decidedly moralistic view of the practices that went hand in hand with American westward expansion, decrying in particular the slaughter of the buffalo. To Roosevelt, the destruction of animal species was a behavior that could not be rewarded, a sentiment Grinnell shared. The two founded the Boone and Crockett Club with the purpose of teaching the morality of hunting culture and preserving what they regarded as the sporting ethos of big-game hunting.

The Boone and Crockett Club was a reaction to the declining number of big-game animals in the West and a way to castigate the commercial hunting culture of the era. Grinnell and Roosevelt, scions of the American aristocracy, were appalled by the application of technology to commercial hunting and innovations such as huge-muzzled punt guns, which allowed the indiscriminate killing of masses of waterfowl. Grinnell had earlier applied his influence to the preservation of the few remaining buffalo, railing against the lack of protection for the species even in Yellowstone National Park. He and Roosevelt used their club and the stature of their members as a tool of moral suasion in an effort to preserve decimated species.

By the 1890s the concept of wildlife preservation enjoyed favor with a good many Americans of wealth and privilege— but far less credence with those who made their living from the land. The issue divided Americans by wealth and class. The attitude of Roosevelt, Grinnell, and others like them soon became part of the mainstream of American conservation; many more less influential people—immigrants, rural Americans, and others who saw in hunting birds and game food, power over at least this aspect of their lives—did not understand how men and women whose fortunes came from similar activities in earlier generations could oppose their meager efforts to enrich themselves and their families. This issue of hunting regulation produced one of the early manifestations of class in American conservation.

At the time, people of wealth and privilege usually had their way in American society, and the development of legal protection for animals and birds serves as a case in point. The Lacey Act of 1894 first specified jail sentences as punishment for the wanton destruction of game birds within the boundaries of Yellowstone National Park. That a national park would be sacrosanct, a place protected from hunting, seemed an obvious assumption to later generations, but before 1894 no piece of legislation had made clear that distinction. The United States Army administered Yellowstone, and when its officers arrested and attempted to prosecute people who entered the vast park with the intent of killing birds and animals for their own use, they found there were no laws suited to this purpose. Congressman John F. Lacey of Iowa, an early and ardent friend of conservation who chaired the House Public Lands Committee, sponsored the first piece of federal legislation that secured protection for nonhuman species.

Lacey's second piece of powerful conservation legislation, the watershed Lacey Act of 1900, marked the beginning of federal wildlife policy. It permitted the secretary of agriculture to take measures to preserve, distribute, reintroduce, and restore game birds and wild birds as long as the secretary's rules did not infringe upon the authority of the states. The bill also created penalties for transporting illegally killed birds across state lines. In this the Lacey Act foreshadowed a more complicated future, in which the class-based goals of the conservation movement grappled with the needs of poor people who subsisted on the bounty of public land.

The Lacey Act of 1900 was a harbinger of the future. Like other similar pieces of legislation, it strongly hinted at the force of the conservation idea as the twentieth century approached. But the strands that became the movement remained largely independent of one another. Lacey took an increasingly visible role in sponsoring legislation, and Roosevelt and Grinnell and their friends and the people who supported archaeological protection often summered at the same resorts, but few seemed to recognize that a conceptual framework linked wildlife protection, forest and water conservation, and the preservation of prehistory. In an era of agrarian revolt, when farmers sought to monetarize silver to help their economic prospects and the nation wallowed in a debilitating economic depression (from 1893 to 1897), the concerns of the conservation constituency seemed at odds with the major issues of the day.

The politics of the era also inhibited the rise of conservation. After 1865 Republican presidents served all but Grover Cleveland's two separate terms, 1884–1888 and 1892–1896, and most were closely tied to railroads or other large industrial concerns that dominated the nation. The 1896 election of William McKinley confirmed the situation. An Ohioan, McKinley was beholden to Marcus A. Hanna, the political boss of the state, which was one of the nation's most industrialized. McKinley opposed the monetarization of silver, which would have aided agrarian debtors; he and his supporters were called "gold bugs" and wore bug-shaped gold pins on their lapels to indicate their political persuasion. With the Boy Orator of the Platte, William Jennings Bryan, seeking to wrest the presidency from the Republicans and securing 46 percent of the popular vote in 1896, McKinley and his supporters looked to industry for the money and influence to complete their victory. When he took office, the new president had little time for even those of wealth and privilege who advocated conservation.

But the dawn of the new century meant new concerns. The

stage was set for organized conservation, though the mechanisms of government and society had not yet come together.
Luminaries such as John Muir and Gifford Pinchot, the first
American trained in forestry, attracted popular attention, and
the public began to develop an awareness of places such as the
Grand Canyon and Yellowstone National Park; but nothing
moved it toward action. By the end of the 1890s a cadre of activists had fashioned the currents that would become conservation. They lacked only a galvanizing force. Theodore
Roosevelt became that catalyst when in 1901 he ascended to
the White House.

2

Progressive Conservation

ALMOST BY ACCIDENT, within William McKinley's second administration was the man who changed turn-of-the-century American reform from a series of loose strands into the configuration labeled progressivism. Theodore Roosevelt was an unlikely candidate to be McKinley's vice president; a man of standing and principle, he was already at odds with the business-as-usual style of the turn-of-the-century Republican party. His friends—and enemies—sought the vice presidency for him, the friends as a tribute to his achievements and his integrity, the enemies as a way to marginalize him in a prestigious but insignificant role. Only a few Republican stalwarts recognized the danger in this strategy. When the forty-two-year-old New Yorker was selected for the vice presidency, Mark Hanna, McKinley's political mentor, growled at his peers: "Don't any of you realize that there's only one life between that madman and the presidency?"

McKinley's assassination at the Pan-American Exposition in Buffalo, New York, in 1901 proved Hanna correct. It catapulted Roosevelt to the presidency, where he promptly showed an administration with all the traits mainstream Republicans feared. Known for his strong views well before he entered national politics, Roosevelt personified the vigorous United States that was reaching maturity as the twentieth century approached. He was energetic, resourceful, determined, and absolutely sure he was right. His arrogance matched that of his nation, signaling America's emergence as a world power. Roosevelt used the presidency as a bully pulpit, proudly trumpeting his beliefs. One of his first actions as president took aim at the oldest of American taboos. As his first month as chief executive ended, Roosevelt invited Booker T. Washington to dinner at the White House. Washington was the first African American to sit as a guest of the president, a gesture that enraged the South and set the tone for the complicated and contentious manner in which Roosevelt governed.

Roosevelt's personal history shaped the way he led the nation. A member of the patrician class who became the first person of his background to choose public service as a career, Roosevelt battled corruption wherever he found it. As civil service commissioner during the administration of President Benjamin Harrison, he tried to jail the president's political patron. As New York City's police commissioner, he battled corruption in Gotham. He wrote literary criticism and prize-winning histories, including the six-volume *The Winning of the West*, earning respect as one of the best-known writers of his time. As assistant secretary of the navy, he spoiled for a war with Spain, the last colonial power in the Americas. When he took his Rough Riders up San Juan Hill in the Spanish-American War, he became the symbol of his age. By 1900, when he became vice president, Roosevelt had accomplished more than most people could in a lifetime.

T.R., as he was often called, enjoyed a healthy appreciation of nature, a trait he shared at the start of the new century with most Americans of his class. But there was a pronounced difference between him and his peers: Roosevelt had overcome adversity in his own life. Asthmatic and sickly as a youth, he grew to advocate the strenuous life. After the death of his wife and his mother in the same house in a twenty-four-hour period in 1883, Roosevelt moved west, to the Dakotas, and hardened himself against physical and psychological frailty. There he acquired genuine experience in a still untamed world. When he arrived in the Dakotas he was, he confessed to a companion, "most anxious to get into a buckskin suit," but he carried the derisive nickname "Four Eyes." In a mythic story he retold throughout his life, he earned his position in the West with the power of a right-led combination of punches. It made him into "Old Four Eyes," a term of respect rather than derision.

For Roosevelt, still in his twenties, the Western landscape became the canvas on which he reinvented himself. To this young man still finding the sources of his power, his experience as rancher and cowman brought him rebirth. He was remade from the morass of modernity into an independent, intellectually and physically self-sufficient being who had learned to endure. In this sense he mirrored the strivings of the nation, a pattern that continued through his years in the White House. For this man often described as having been born with his mind made up, renewal was a source of power, a yardstick of authenticity by which he measured himself and all others. If you could endure, you could survive in Roosevelt's world.

Roosevelt's presidency was marked by the implementation of a national reform program called the "Square Deal." Three spheres drew the president's attention: he wanted to regulate business, protect the public, and create discernible standards for decision-making in American society. During the seven years he served as president, Roosevelt regulated interstate commerce, implemented child labor laws, created agencies to ensure quality and cleanliness in food production, attacked the trusts that dominated the American economic scene, and generally watched out for the welfare of the public in ways that his predecessors had not. The Justice Department's antitrust suit against the Northern Securities Company, which

controlled all the railroad lines between Seattle and Min-
neapolis, revealed the president's priorities. Roosevelt differ-
entiated between what he saw as "good" and "bad" trusts,
those that hurt the public and those that were necessary because of the new size and scale of the American economy.
Only the trusts he labeled "bad" were his target, and the
Northern Securities Company was one. The Meat Inspection
Act, which created government regulation of meat manufacture and meat packing, and the Pure Food and Drug Act of
1906, which regulated the quality of food and drugs in interstate commerce, exemplified his efforts to protect the public.
In both these areas, the Roosevelt administration won notable
success.

Nowhere did Roosevelt leave a greater mark than in the
nascent field of conservation, where science was applied to the
problems of supply in American society. The president was
well tuned to the message of a finite world. Better than any
other American, he intuited the import of the frontier's
closing and admired and sympathized with John Muir.
Embodying the complicated impulses of turn-of-the-century
conservation, Roosevelt often said that he learned his conservation principles from Gifford Pinchot. In the end, Roosevelt
came down on Pinchot's side. He believed that scientific management of resources could set the nation on a surer footing.
Ordered, rational decision-making could prevent scarcity and
the problems that would certainly stem from it. He embraced
the ideal of professionalism, already making itself felt
throughout American society. Efficiency could only come
from the knowledge of trained experts, who applied objective,
science-based solutions to modern problems.

In this way conservation shared the Progressive movement's goals and its many inherent tensions. Conservation
possessed clear centralizing tendencies. It offered a system, a
way of looking at the world that impressed values, ideas, and

programs, usually based in science or a scientific rationale, on society. Conservation created order from chaos, an order clearly defined, measured, and demonstrable. It relied on law instead of community sanction to set boundaries, demonstrating its roots in industrial, urban society. In the crowded, anonymous world that writers such as the urban social realist Theodore Dreiser, author of *Sister Carrie*, offered to their audiences, law rather than contemporary mores defined the limits of social interaction.

The idea of using law to centralize power in the hands of the responsible few challenged the larger American ethos of local control and became one of the most important battlegrounds in American history. Progressivism and conservation reprised an age-old American tension between two of the words in the name of the nation: "united" and "states." One represented the centralized power of the federal government, ascendant with the advent of the Roosevelt administration; the other stood for local control, the historic mode of the American republic. Against the backdrop of an urban industrial society, these tensions, along with those between the individual and society, played themselves out. Those who believed in individual primacy found themselves faced with a society in which most of the power structure seemed determined to impress a set of rules that regulated behavior. In the struggle between self and society, conservation stood as a symbol of the idea of community, of a greater good rather than individual enrichment. At the turn of the century, that position made conservation a bellwether of progressivism.

In the upheaval that Progressive reform brought to American society, no area of behavior was more challenged than traditional attitudes toward the natural world. Americans had always regarded the physical world as infinite. They cut trees at will, for timber seemed to stretch as far as the eye could see.

They hunted any animal they saw, for these too seemed abundant beyond belief. They proudly used land until they used it up. Old farmers might boast of how they wore out three farms in their lifetime, a way of confirming their energy and zeal, and their peers cheered their achievements. America was a land of plenty, and its people lived with the assurance that they could do whatever they wanted in the natural world.

As newly professionalized scientists stood at its helm, Progressive conservation presented a direct challenge to this older ethos. One of its primary dimensions was the idea of efficiency, which offered methodical, systematic remedies as the solution to the widespread sense that Americans were running out of natural resources. Management for the long term, for the greatest good for the greatest number in the long run, was essential to the strangely limited egalitarianism embodied in this doctrine. Resources were to be used wisely for the benefit of all. A narrow group of specialists, who shared class and economic background, made the decisions that shaped those uses.

These contradictory ideas became the watchwords of conservation. Closely tied to progressivism, its twin in values, goals, and even contradictions, conservation embodied the emergence of a middle-class society based in the industrial revolution that ironically seemed to reach for a preindustrial past. Politically bipartisan in character, the loosely knit collection of professionals and concerned citizens who became conservationists shared most of the traits of progressivism. They favored public solutions over private ones, entrusted a core group of experts with the authority to make decisions that affected everyone's future, and viewed the world in decidedly middle-class terms. Yet there were important distinctions among the community of professionals, and they were revealed in the response to maladies that stemmed from industrialization.

The battle over the response to water pollution exemplified both the rise of professionalism and the competition between different groups of experts for control of the conservation process. The vast post-1865 expansion of American industry fouled air, water, and land, and by the beginning of the Progressive era, conservationists looked for ways to limit pollution. Water loomed large in this formulation, for land still seemed abundant and air pollution often had been successfully allayed by higher and higher smokestacks—which spewed waste over larger areas, limiting its impact in any single place. The lethal cholera epidemics of 1832, 1849, and 1866 remained bitter memories, though, and industrial water pollution presented a threat to the safety of people in cities as well as an affront to the professionals who assumed an increasingly important role in American society.

The response to water pollution began as a check on waterborne diseases. Beginning in 1878 in Massachusetts, large industrial states passed water-quality laws. Upriver users who dumped waste into rivers were held liable in the courts, and by 1905 more than thirty-five states listed water pollution laws on their books. State boards of health administered the laws. By the 1890s, after scientists demonstrated how typhoid fever was transmitted in sewage, purification of waste became a singular goal of the reformers. It was as if by cleaning water they might remove the stain of an unchecked society.

In one of the most telling cases, public health became the battleground between competing professional cultures. Thanks to rapid industrial growth, the Pittsburgh, Pennsylvania, area exceeded a million people early in the twentieth century. In the 1880s the municipality had constructed a sewage system that by 1909 covered 538 miles. The system released untreated sewage into the Allegheny, Monongahela, and Ohio rivers, creating a serious public health problem. Cities down river from points of discharge, including Pittsburgh, drew their drinking water from the rivers. Among other consequences, the untreated sewage led to raging epidemics of typhoid fever which never seemed entirely to disappear. In 1905 Pittsburgh built a sand filtration system that by 1908 reduced the city's typhoid death rate from 100 to 22 per 100,000 people. Although the new system clearly demonstrated the link between fouled drinking water and typhoid fever, it did little for the people downstream. They continued to draw their water from the rivers into which Pittsburgh dumped its untreated sewage, and faced ongoing typhoid epidemics.

Efforts to address this problem pitted two professional groups against each other—the physicians who set up state boards of health, and the sanitary engineers who devised solutions to the engineering problems of industrialization. Both groups represented the future, the culture of progress. Both required degrees of their practitioners, observed professional standards, and embodied the idea that trained professionals would provide solutions to the problems of progress. Both believed that their method would solve the sewage problems that beset not only Pittsburgh but every other industrial city.

Yet the two groups had different ideas about how to overcome the problems of waste in water. Sanitary engineers claimed they would succeed because they understood the limitations of municipal financing, while physicians asserted that only they, as trained specialists in curing disease, could satisfactorily address the question. The two groups advocated very different strategies. Progressive-era physicians often took a reformer's stand. They recommended that cities act to prevent untreated sewage from ending up in waterways. In 1907 a medical representative of the Pennsylvania Board of Health indicated that the policy of the state was to "bring about the abandonment of streams as carriers of sewage." The absolute standard they often promoted—pollution-free streams—was expensive and hard to achieve, but in the minds of physicians, well worth it. Sanitary engineers regarded waste disposal in waterways as an economic question as well as a health concern that needed to be resolved at the local level on a case-by-case basis. There was no absolute standard of purity, engineers averred, and the search for one only slowed the process of addressing the problem.

For a range of reasons, the sanitary engineers triumphed. The cost of treating sewage to achieve absolute purity was staggering, and city managers and others were pleased to have a sliding scale that nonetheless carried professional sanction. Sanitary engineers offered a guarantee by science that absolute purity was not essential. Their professional standing, and the reflexive view that science and truth were the same thing, meant that sanitary engineers could be believed. The struggle to determine sewage management in Pittsburgh became one of the first cases in which competing sciences represented differing points of view on a question of public health. Professional knowledge was not always the panacea that Progressives thought it to be. Instead the case of sewage in Pittsburgh revealed the ways in which competing professional standards could be substituted for the arbitrary distinctions of the Gilded Age. Science triumphed, but not a science of absolute values. Instead Progressives settled for a technical solution: water that was clean enough to drink without the threat of epidemic disease, but that could still carry waste away from cities. The case established a precedent that reigned for more than a generation.

As Theodore Roosevelt came to represent the many strands of reform generally, Gifford Pinchot stood in the forefront of conservation. Born in New York in 1865 into a wealthy family that had made its fortune in land speculation and development, Pinchot was raised to be a powerful man and lived his life on those terms. His father, James, began his career as a timberman in the Upper Delaware Valley, engaging in the practices of the time: clear-cutting forests and leaving behind denuded hills, eroded terrain, and silted rivers. Later in life, James Pinchot questioned not only the practice of clear-cutting but his culture's understanding of the human use of the natural world. He embraced the ethic of professionalism and the reliance on objective science long before such ideas swept the country. As part of this reevaluation, as a way of doing his part to heal the land, James Pinchot urged his eldest son to train for a career as a professional forester.

Gifford Pinchot took this counsel to heart and became the first American trained in forestry. After graduating from Yale University he studied at L'Ecole Nationale Forestière, the national forestry institute at Nancy, France. As he learned the professional techniques of the age, grasped the concept of silviculture—forestry as a crop, managed to guarantee a fixed annual supply of trees ready for cutting—and marveled at the right-angled roads through the managed forests of France, he also recognized that scientific forestry was a business, a lucrative and socially significant one. In Europe, Pinchot learned that despite the enormous number of trees in the United States and the widely held sense that they would last forever, Americans needed to manage their timber to avoid shortages.

Pinchot also made one other important intellectual connection in Europe, the link between scientific efficiency and equity. During a visit to Germany he was appalled by the hierarchical nature of European forestry, by the way in which foresters were closely identified with power and privilege and regarded as overseers by the people of the land. European forestry might be an extension of the power of kings and barons, but in the New World, Pinchot asserted, forestry would take on the democratic characteristics of American society. In this sentiment he was closely linked to Teddy Roosevelt, Frederick Jackson Turner, and the emerging ethic of Progressive conservation.

After his return to the United States in 1890, Pinchot established himself as a consulting forester and practiced forestry much as an attorney would practice law. This seemingly odd choice of occupation—hanging out a shingle that said "Gifford Pinchot, Consulting Forester" in New York City and expecting business to walk through the door—survived at first in no small part due to Pinchot's personal and familial connections and the general move toward professionalism in American society. Pinchot possessed one of the most important attributes of his time, professional training in his field of choice, and his first client, George W. Vanderbilt, was a family friend. On Vanderbilt's Biltmore estate outside of Asheville, North Carolina, Pinchot applied the techniques of managed forestry, and in the first year turned a small profit. This demonstration (with little at stake; after all, Biltmore cared not a whit whether Pinchot made a profit) proved the point: forestry could be efficient, equitable, and profitable while guaranteeing a continuous source of timber.

When he took over the Division of Forestry in the U.S. Department of Agriculture in 1898, Pinchot applied the same ideas to the vast expanses of federally managed forests. Federal forestry was a swamp of competing interests, and the bureau Pinchot inherited had no particularly bright prospects. With an intuitive understanding of public relations, he set about carving a clear place for scientific forestry, not only in the federal bureaucracy but also with the American public at large. His connections, education, and wealth gave him the opportunity to make his case to the most powerful segments of American society, and his passionate beliefs about the significance of forestry won him considerable respect. With this advance Pinchot became the quintessential Progressive, as clearly identified with reform as Theodore Roosevelt.

Pinchot and Roosevelt were two of a kind, the first individuals of their patrician background engaged in public service, and Roosevelt's ascent to the presidency catapulted Pinchot to great prominence. The two enjoyed a close relationship, Roosevelt mentoring Pinchot and showering so much attention on him that the young forester became known as the "crown prince" of the Roosevelt administration. Pinchot always had the president's ear, a situation that made him the envy of many and the enemy of others. If there was a faster way to get information to Teddy Roosevelt than through Pinchot, few knew of it.

Pinchot added a new dimension to the reform movement and especially to conservation. While reform had been prominent, many reformers spoke mostly to others who already embraced their cause. Pinchot had an intuitive understanding of public relations and helped spread the message of progressivism. In conservation he took the existing dimensions of forestry—science and economics—and added what became the dominant art of the twentieth century, politics. It was a heady and powerful combination for a man who turned forty in 1905, the same year he engineered the consolidation of federal forests under the control of the new U.S. Forest Service in the Department of Agriculture. Pinchot became its first chief.

No federal agency more clearly exemplified the Progressive impulse than did Pinchot's Forest Service. The agency thoroughly subscribed to the cornucopia of ideas that made up progressivism. Like Woodrow Wilson, who as president of Princeton University dedicated his institution to the nation's service, Pinchot engineered a name change from "Bureau of Forestry" to "United States Forest Service" to reflect the importance of service in its mission. He trumpeted science and insisted on efficiency, as did nearly all Progressive leaders, and his axiom, "The greatest good for the greatest number in the long run," reflected the obsession with equity that was the

Progressive response to the vast power of individual wealth in
late-nineteenth-century America. Pinchot's supple handling
of the timber industry, his firm commitment to conservation
goals, and his close relationship with Roosevelt combined to
make the Forest Service stand out among federal bureaus at
the turn of the century.

The Forest Service enjoyed one major distinction from
other Progressive bureaucracies: despite Pinchot's position at
its absolute center, the agency strove for decentralization in an
increasingly centralized world. Pinchot advocated management from the ground level. He made policy in Washington,
D.C., and then the men his emissaries selected implemented it
on the ground. Initially these men were drawn from communities near the national forests—as the forest reserves were
called after 1905. Those who commanded the respect of their
neighbors, who demonstrated prowess at forestry skills, and
who seemed to understand the idea of conservation were chosen to manage more than a million acres of timber for a salary
of $80 per month. Forestry schools proliferated after 1900, evi-
dence of the concept of service, the success of the idea of conservation, and the professionalization of American society.
Their graduates came to the woods, bringing comprehensive
training in forestry if not always a healthy respect for local
practice. Their guide was always the *Use Book*, a 4-1/4 by
6-3/4-inch compendium of the rules and regulations of the
agency that governed individual decision-making. Time and
again, foresters in the field bent the rules and found ways to
accommodate local people. This was the price of decentralization in a centralized era, the ongoing tension between what
was ideal and what was possible a thousand miles from Forest
Service headquarters in Washington, D.C.

Pinchot reigned at the Forest Service until 1910, when he
was ousted in the so-called Ballinger-Pinchot controversy.
The transfer of power from Roosevelt to William Howard

Taft complicated Pinchot's position. During the Roosevelt administration he had enjoyed great freedom and considerable power; Taft had his own inner circle, and Pinchot was excluded. It seemed to Pinchot that Taft weakened the protection of public lands, especially in regard to hydroelectric development. When Taft allowed his secretary of the interior Richard A. Ballinger to reduce federal supervision of power interests, Pinchot was outraged. From his position in the Department of Agriculture, a separate entity beyond Ballinger's control, Pinchot became a leading critic of administration policy and of Ballinger. In 1910 he accused Ballinger of assisting in inappropriate transfers of coal-laden public lands in Alaska to a private syndicate. When President Taft sided with Ballinger and fired Pinchot, it closed Pinchot's federal career.

As long as Pinchot remained at its head, the Forest Service remained the dominant federal land management agency. It stood at the forefront not only of conservation but also of Progressive reform, exemplifying what the American people at the turn of the century regarded as the best impulses of government and society. The Forest Service truly had at heart the idea of the greatest good for the greatest number in the long run—as long as that greatest number comprised the people who counted at the turn of the century, the American middle class. Conservation, like progressivism as a whole, embodied an important contradiction. While it had a greater good in mind, it was no more inclusive than any other movement in turn-of-the-century America.

Federal bureaus offered one mechanism for Progressive conservation, but equally as important, conservationists put their faith in legislative remedies. The middle-class supporters of conservation had great faith in law as a means for regulating human behavior. Conservationists advocated something gen-

uinely new in the American experience. Since the European
discovery of the New World, people—from fishermen to
farmers to loggers—had treated the natural world with im-
punity. Conservation taught, indeed preached, a new and different ethic, using the most basic form of prohibition: law.
Like most Progressives, conservationists believed in the goodwill of the citizenry and their respect for American institutions. With hindsight they were easy to regard as naive: they
truly believed that if the government passed a law, people
would abide by it because it was the law and because law was
just.

As a result, legislation defined Progressive conservation.
From the Reclamation Act of 1902 to the Antiquities Act of
1906, conservation became part of a legal revolution that reflected the values of progressivism and the growing popular
sentiment behind it. Law served as the means to promote the
morality of the day and seemed to Progressives the best available remedy for social problems.

Of the issues that attracted conservationists, water supply
became one of the most important. Much of the late nineteenth century had been devoted to settling the American
West, and much of that region was semi-arid or arid. Unlike
the Eastern, more humid area of the nation, where annual
rainfall could support agriculture, the arid West experienced
inconsistent rainfall at the wrong times of the year. Agriculture in the West would require other water sources. Before
1900 innovators such as John Wesley Powell investigated irrigation, and private companies developed irrigation projects.
In 1888, near Roswell, New Mexico, Pat Garrett, who as sher-
iff of Lincoln County had shot and killed the notorious outlaw
William "Billy the Kid" Bonney in 1880, developed a major
irrigation project. By the mid-1890s most private companies
had gone bust, and the West looked to the federal government
as a source of irrigation funding.

Public interest and federal laws that already supported irrigation combined to make it one of the major issues of the 1890s. The Carey Act of 1894 granted each Western state one million acres of federal land which could be sold to raise funds for irrigation projects. Buffalo Bill Cody, the famed Western hero and showman, attempted the largest endeavor, a project of more than 500,000 acres in Wyoming's Big Horn Basin. It had limited success. Private investors were not thrilled with its prospects nor with those of many other proposed projects. By the end of the decade the clamor for further federal legislation grew louder. A young California attorney, George H. Maxwell, spearheaded this drive. In 1896 he persuaded the National Irrigation Congress—and in later years the National Board of Trade, the National Business Men's League, and the National Association of Manufacturers—to support federal involvement in irrigation. After learning of the *acequias*, the democratic communal irrigation channels of Hispanic New Mexico, William E. Smythe became another passionate advocate of irrigation. He founded *Irrigation Age*, the leading magazine of the field, which spoke out editorially for federal support. In 1899 Maxwell organized another lobbying body, the National Irrigation Association, to further the cause. By 1900 the campaign had succeeded. Both major political parties included support for federal irrigation projects in their platforms.

Among elected officials, Nevada congressman Francis G. Newlands took the lead in supporting irrigation. Born in Mississippi in 1848, Newlands was educated in the East and came to California in 1870 to practice law. He moved to Nevada in 1889 to manage the affairs of his deceased father-in-law, William Sharon, a Nevada mining baron, and became a leader of the mining-rich but population-poor state. Nevada entered the union in 1864 with a small population, which later in the century dwindled to a minuscule number. Newlands believed irrigated land would help bring people back to his state, and federal irrigation became his most important refrain after his 1892 election to Congress.

Westerners both fought and embraced the idea of federally funded water projects. Private ones mostly failed, leaving huge debts and uncomfortable circumstances, but many Westerners feared government involvement in the region. Yet without water, Western boosters had little to promote. Community formation and prosperity depended on consistent water, and the only entity that seemed able to deliver it was the federal government. Generally, by about 1900, Westerners supported the idea of federal irrigation out of necessity, in effect holding their figurative noses while insisting that their representatives push for legislation.

Efforts to replace private reclamation with federal projects also drew Eastern support, though not typically from the working people who many supposed would benefit from its provisions. Instead it was Eastern manufacturers who provided most of the support—they expected to sell goods in an expanding agrarian West. Astute businessmen recognized in expanded reclamation the opportunity both to profit and to extend their economic sway.

In 1901 Newlands initiated legislation designed to finance federal irrigation with the proceeds from the sale of Western public lands. It established a revolving fund of revenue from the sale of public land that would be dedicated to the construction of major reclamation projects in the West. Water users were given ten years to repay these construction costs, presumably with the profits from irrigated land, and the money was to be returned to the fund to finance additional projects. The bill also allowed settlers to homestead these lands but limited the portion of an individual homestead that could be irrigated with federal water to 160 acres. The limit was designed to promote family farms, both to spur population growth in states such as Nevada—another of Newlands's goals—and to settle the West with people that turn-of-the-century Americans regarded as the backbone of their society—landowning agriculturalists, yeoman farmers in the Jeffersonian tradition.

In this sense the Newlands Act, as the reclamation bill was called, was a perfect Progressive project. Government dollars fused scientific knowledge and the control it provided over the physical world with the egalitarianism of the family farm. By creating landowners who inhabited the West, by empowering people, a government project would help build a more independent, more powerful America. Reclamation was science in the service of people, one of the highest ideals of progressivism. No wonder the project was close to Theodore Roosevelt's heart. On its surface it fit every Progressive objective.

Despite the best intentions, reclamation did not fulfill the social objectives of Progressive conservation. Large parcels of the public domain did not become family farms. In some instances, such as the Salt River project in Arizona, which began in 1905, the Reclamation Service—after 1923 known as the Bureau of Reclamation—irrigated private land simply to receive credit for a successful project. Nor were all irrigated public lands desirable. Neither the children of Western farmers nor the urban poor lined up to homestead irrigated land, and over time large landowners and, later, corporate farms received much of the new water. Powerful bureaucracies and influence-wielding corporate interests grew up in place of the egalitarian agricultural society that John Wesley Powell, Francis Newlands, and others had envisioned.

Although reclamation granted federal agencies considerable power, it was popular in the West. Other federal efforts inspired regional ire. Roosevelt played an important role in antagonizing Western interests. Between 1901 and 1907 he tripled the amount of land reserved in national forests, from fewer than 50 million acres to more than 150 million acres. Roosevelt's stance so angered Western senators and representatives that in 1907, in consort with Eastern conservatives, they blocked the president from proclaiming additional national forests in Oregon, Idaho, Washington, Montana, and Colorado. Always up to the challenge and sure he was correct, Roosevelt signed this prohibitory legislation with one final tweak: a day earlier he created 21 new national forests. Typical of the man, he showed how the power of the chief executive could be used.

No piece of legislation invested more power in the presidency than did the Antiquities Act of 1906. Passed in response to the wholesale pillaging of archaeological ruins in the Southwest, the imprecise language of the act made it an unparalleled tool in the hands of presidents such as Roosevelt. Although congressional advocates had insisted that the act would apply only to the 160-acre sections surrounding archaeological ruins on public lands, the bill in fact gave the president great leeway. It contained no limits on executive authority to reserve public land, declaring only that their size "be limited to the proper care and management" of the "objects of scientific or historic interest" that were reserved. As a result, the president was presented with unchecked discretion over any portion of the public domain.

The Antiquities Act came to prominence in 1907, when Congress ended the president's power to proclaim national forests in a number of Western states. Before then, it had been used only to proclaim archaeological and natural areas of very limited area. Most of the first ten national monuments, the category of sites created under the Antiquities Act, were tiny. Only Petrified Forest National Monument in Arizona was greater than fifteen thousand acres; most early national monuments were far smaller. During the first eighteen months after its passage, the Antiquities Act did not appear to be an unusual or controversial piece of legislation.

The proclamation of the Grand Canyon National Monument changed that perception. On January 11, 1908, Roosevelt established 806,400 acres of the Grand Canyon as a national monument. With one stroke of his pen he reserved an area so vast as to defy the expectations of even the most avid supporter of the Antiquities Act. The president responded to the threat that a local man planned a tramway from the rim to the bottom of the Grand Canyon. The rim was dotted with mining claims, which were typically used to cater to the tourists brought by the railroad, which first reached the canyon in 1901. An icon that was sacred to turn-of-the-century Americans faced privatization at a moment when the nation favored public over private solutions. Only Roosevelt, armed with the Antiquities Act, stood in the way.

With his proclamation the president revealed the breadth of this seemingly innocuous law. Since 1907, when he lost the power to reserve forest lands in most of the West, Roosevelt had chafed under the watch of a disgruntled Congress. The Antiquities Act allowed him to circumvent the legislature, to move around both the opposition and the fundamentally slow nature of congressional deliberations, to achieve results in an instant that he believed were in the best interests of the public. While Roosevelt did not actually expand the powers of the Antiquities Act, he took full advantage of its provisions and certainly set precedents that extended its range. On his last day in office in 1909 he reserved more than 630,000 acres of the Olympic Peninsula in Washington State as the Mount Olympus National Monument. With that proclamation, Roosevelt gave his enemies in Congress one final jab as he headed out the door.

Roosevelt's application of a vague law created the most effective conservation tool ever enacted as American legislation.

National monuments became the category of choice in numerous situations: when a threat to public land loomed large, when Congress refused to act or opposed a conservation measure, and when land would clearly be valuable to the nation's future even if it had no such claim in the present. With the Antiquities Act, a president had tremendous discretion. Congress could not hold the chief executive hostage in conservation matters, could not force a compromise on an unwilling president, and could not prevent a president from implementing an agenda on public land—with or without congressional approval. Monuments such as the Grand Canyon later became national parks, creating a pattern in which monuments were established in advance of congressional support for their establishment as national parks. These "waystation monuments" now comprise many of the most cherished units in the national park system.

The Antiquities Act embodied all things Progressive. It centralized power in the hands of those who could be trusted, advocated a shared vision of American society (the name "national monument" clearly reflected a vision of the Progressive nation), and relied on experts to make determinations that had once been made by locals. In these ways it followed the Progressive ethic: it centralized power in the hands of the self-proclaimed responsible few, to be exercised in the name of those they regarded as the people. If the law and the people who made it seemed arrogant, it was because they reflected the wholehearted confidence of the time: they knew best, and they sought only the best for all.

In the end, the Antiquities Act gave the conservation movement a powerful tool in the hands of a willing president. Alone it created a legal revolution. Together with a profusion of conservation and related reform legislation, it became part of an upheaval in American society, a transformation of the way Americans accomplished their goals. The Progressives gave law new standing—with everything from the idea of good government to the Pure Food and Drug Act—and conservation often became a beneficiary. No longer would the law be only the tool of the wealthy. The cynical might call law the tool of the middle class, but Progressives, ever smug in their self-righteousness, were certain they had the interests of their entire society in mind.

This legal revolution created a new struggle between competing ideas of what was good for society. The law was malleable and competing interests, all at least middle class, could orchestrate law and policy to suit their needs. In the name of protecting resources, law could divest local hunters in the Adirondacks of New York, subsistence fishermen on the Illinois River, and Hispanic sheepherders in New Mexico of their right to engage in generation-old systems of living. Driven by legalistic, class-based moralism, conservationists worried little about the plight of these dispossessed hunters, farmers, and herders. National objectives triumphed over local concerns, creating powerful class tensions in many regions of the country.

When different reform factions collided, fissures appeared in the conservation movement and indeed in larger areas of reform. People who shared allegiance to the concepts of reform and conservation found that their objectives in specific cases differed. Simply put, they placed higher value on different sides of the same question, leading to contentiousness and acrimony among conservationists that threatened to fracture the loose alliance and negate the gains that stemmed from two decades of concern and a decade of legislation.

The Hetch-Hetchy controversy highlighted this problem. A valley in Yosemite National Park, Hetch-Hetchy was prized for its beauty. It also had fabulous potential as a reservoir for the city of San Francisco, long beset by water problems. In the aftermath of the terrible earthquake of April

1906, which destroyed the city, private water companies stepped into the void. They proposed to stand in place of a municipal utility, in effect contracting to serve a semi-official function as purveyors of water. The companies moved aggressively. One, the North Coast Water Company, run by a nephew of Francis Newlands, sought to build a reservoir and sell water to the city. The younger Newlands faced only one problem: the land the company coveted was one of the last stands of intact redwoods in the entire San Francisco Bay Area and belonged to U.S. Representative William Kent, an ardent conservationist. Recognizing that in the aftermath of the earthquake any court in the region would favor North Coast's condemnation suit, Kent gave the land to the United States under the terms of the Antiquities Act, offering the name Muir Woods for the national monument his gift created.

The private water companies continued to press for opportunities to convert public resources to their private gain. In another instance the San Joaquin Water Company proposed to blow up Devil's Postpile, a huge basalt formation adjacent to the San Joaquin River that had been excised from Yosemite National Park in 1904, and use its rubble to dam the river. They too planned to sell the water to San Francisco. The Sierra Club became involved and, using its political influence, arranged for the establishment of the Devil's Postpile National Monument. Again, public-minded civic action thwarted private endeavor.

With these events as background, the struggle for Hetch-Hetchy took on greater importance. Hetch-Hetchy remained within Yosemite National Park, but it was the city of San Francisco, not private interests, that now sought to convert it to a reservoir. A seven-year battle over the dam pitted long-time friends such as Muir and Kent against one another—a few years after his gift of the woods in Muir's name, Kent said of his friend's stance against the dam: Muir "has no social sense, with him, it is God and the rock where God put it and that is the end of the story"—and bitterly divided conservationists such as Pinchot from preservation advocates like Muir. The struggle challenged many of the placid assumptions of the idea of conservation. Utilitarian conservation and the preservation goals of John Muir were not always compatible. In the end, when the U.S. Senate approved the dam at Hetch-Hetchy, the concept of conservation gained a triumph at the expense not of rapacious users of resources but of its preservationist allies. By 1914 the dam was in place, inundating the valley after revealing the inherent divisions in the broader concept of conservation.

Hetch-Hetchy became the pivotal moment in early conservation, the time when the different strains of the movement found they had less in common than it seemed when they faced a hostile outside world. Muir, ever dogmatic, took the position that Hetch-Hetchy was a moral issue. Destroying the valley was desecration on a colossal scale. To those who favored the dam, its construction was truly a practical question. The people of San Francisco needed a dependable supply of water, and municipal government was the best manager. From this perspective, Hetch-Hetchy was an exchange—of beauty and spirituality for opportunity and fairness. It also illustrated that the spread of conservation had made the ideas of some of its founders untenable.

Hetch-Hetchy was also part of the larger context of progressivism. After the failure of private water companies to accomplish the same end in nearby canyons that were not within national park boundaries, San Francisco's success can only be attributed to the bias of the era for public rather than private solutions. The Hetch-Hetchy dam succeeded because the entity that sought it was public. The others failed because they were perceived as private business schemes. In the end, re-

source conservation embodied all the traits of the larger movement from which it was derived.

Elsewhere the benefits of public over private stewardship
were not as apparent. When Los Angeles successfully utilized
its municipal status to drain the water from Owens Valley in
eastern California's Inyo County, the farmers of the valley
took out an advertisement in the *Los Angeles Times* that read:
"We, the farmers of the Owens Valley, who are about to die,
salute you." The transformation enriched private interests
closely tied to the water district, creating a series of power relationships that continued throughout the century. In other
cases, private interests masquerading as public entities, often
comprised of the very people who led public consortiums,
were able to secure water and lock it up in private reservoirs.
In places such as Lake Alamanor in northern California, a
travesty of the Progressive goals was played out. Private entities from San Francisco seized control of the regional water
supply and created a lake, destroying local and regional agriculture and ranching. The result was the creation of an intraregional, in fact intrastate, colony of San Francisco. Again
the biases of progressivism caused as much harm—to people
who were not part of the urban middle class—as it accomplished for others.

Progressive conservation shaped efforts to preserve and
conserve for the better part of a half-century. For better and
for worse, the values of progressivism were part of conservation: efficiency, equity, and social responsibility. Those who
benefited from Progressive conservation were largely members of the urban middle class. Conservation's blind spot obscured the travails of lower-income people and minorities.
The movement's roots were so firmly in the middle class, and
the culture of the time so ignored the woes of others, that it is
easy to regard the movement as the province of the elite. Such
a characterization would not be entirely fair, but in many

ways it struck the mark. Conservationists were people of their time, place, and background. They acted accordingly in designating their goals, devising their strategies, and seizing their opportunities.

3

Conservation as Business and Labor Policy

BETWEEN 1920 and 1945 conservation reflected the dominant ethos in American society. The nation ran from the top down, with decisions made by a small group of leaders, typically Northeastern and affluent, tied to business and enamored of an easy and often opulent small-town life that industrialism had conversely granted much of the nation. In good times its leaders had respect for the values of conservation; in harder times they saw a need to utilize the nation's resources. A bipartisan conservation ethic took hold, geographically dividing the nation between the common interests of the East, on the one hand, and those of the West and South, on the other, rather than reflecting the political stances of the major parties.

Conservation became part of the mainstream, a principle of the classes that led American society, its embrace a marker of belonging in the company of American leaders. During the 1920s, when the nation seemed to break with its past and fashion a new set of urban—and sometimes urbane—values, conservation became an anchor of tradition in American society, a link between past and present, a way to tie together the nation's disparate factions. Conservation also included a business-oriented ethic, a development strategy that applied federal dollars to infrastructure needs. For all its turmoil, the 1920s produced a gentleman's brand of conservation, emanating from the narrow elite and oblivious to the economic, spiritual, and recreational needs of the larger public.

The New Deal transformed conservation into labor policy, but conservation was a by-product rather than an objective in response to the Great Depression of the 1930s. Under the New Deal, conservation programs stood on equal footing with capital development ventures, for both put large numbers of people to work. Franklin Roosevelt's administration did more work on federal land than had been accomplished in the forty years since conservation became a recognized ideal. Some of this involved clearing brush and trees and cutting fire trails, or building roads and other facilities, or transforming the landscape into regulated management. The Tennessee Valley Authority, a regional planning program designed to help the impoverished people of Appalachia, provided another huge component, as did programs to rehabilitate overgrazed Indian reservation land and the Dust Bowl regions of Kansas, Colorado, New Mexico, Oklahoma, and Texas. Conservation required intensive manpower. No commodity existed in greater abundance in 1930s America, where there was less demand for labor than ever before. As a consequence, conservation became one of the most essential employment devices of the era.

America's entry into World War II preempted the pursuit of conservation. The military conscripted men previously assigned to conservation activities, and the demands of waging a global war deflected attention from conservation goals. Rapid industrialization and urbanization created a stronger demand for recreational space, but the dictates of war made such objectives to be wished for rather than acted on. During World War II the ideal of conservation held; it was simply deferred until the crisis passed.

By the end of the war in 1945, a powerful and pervasive

federal bureaucracy, forged by the New Deal and strengthened by the needs of wartime administration, stepped to the
fore in conservation. With the support of gentleman conservationists, these agencies created a world in which they could
implement their objectives without significant concern for opposition. When opponents emerged, professional conservation
organizations leaped to the support of their favorite agencies.
A kind of hegemony was produced that could survive only as
long as conservation remained a specialized interest.

No period has so captured the American imagination as the
1920s. The Jazz Age, as the decade was often called, was defined by divisions: between those who opposed Prohibition
(the outlawing of alcohol) and those who favored it; between
those who embraced the new culture of leisure and those, such
as Ma and Pa Kettle portrayed in Grant Wood's famous paint-
ing *American Gothic*, who clung dearly to traditional values;
and between those who had the means to enjoy the fruits of
industrialization and those who did not. Progressivism became only one of a number of social concepts that contended
for dominance. The battle over the teaching of the theory of
evolution in public schools, waged most prominently in the
Scopes "Monkey Trial," held in Dayton, Tennessee, in 1925,
was only one manifestation of the hold of traditional views of
God, nature, and law on much of the American population.
The radio, moving pictures (as the silent films of the era were
called), and the rise of national advertising all contributed to
the beginnings of national media that influenced mass culture.
The confidence that John Dos Passos had once called the quiet
afterglow of the nineteenth century disappeared in the triumphant tragedy of war and the many voices afterward that
claimed authority.

The values of the era, too, were different. Instead of the social goals that had dominated the Progressive era, the 1920s

seemed possessed by rampant individualism. If the Progressive era stressed collective order, the Jazz Age embodied emotion and individual exploration. New technologies contributed to the shift. By the 1930s researchers in the fictitious "Middletown" (actually Muncie, Indiana) learned that American youth already embraced their own culture, different from that of their elders. It relied on the technologies of the age, especially the automobile, to assure them freedom from detection by their parents. For most Americans in the 1920s, especially urbanites, veterans, and the young, social objectives fell far behind individual goals when they decided what was important.

Conservation could seem old-fashioned in this climate. At the turn of the century it had been closely tied to cultural affirmation, a way of valuing the nation by considering its natural wonders. The impulse to visit the Grand Canyon was as much to revere American culture as to gaze at the great chasm. In the 1920s, individualism and the search for the personal overwhelmed the social goals of conservation. When one could hear the radio broadcast of Harold "Red" Grange's five touchdowns for Illinois against Michigan in 1925, or read in the newspaper about the exploits of Al Capone and about flappers and speakeasies, how could a hike in the woods compete for the attention of the young?

One continuing role for conservation was in the development of a recreational ethos in the national parks. After World War I the park system grew with impressive speed. Under the leadership of Stephen T. Mather, the first director of the National Park Service, and his right-hand man and successor, Horace M. Albright, the agency added many important new park areas. These included the Grand Canyon (Arizona) and Zion (Utah), both of which became national parks in 1919, and Bryce Canyon (Utah) and Grand Teton (Wyoming) national parks in 1928 and 1929. Mather and Albright broadened the park system from its almost exclusively Western focus, adding Lafayette National Park (later renamed Acadia) in Bar Harbor, Maine, in 1919, and in 1926 authorizing three national parks in the Southeast—Great Smoky Mountains, Shenandoah, and Mammoth Cave. From Acadia to Mammoth Cave, the Eastern national parks not only broadened the constituency for the system, they placed national parks in proximity to most Americans. The numbers of people that flooded these "sacred" locations revealed the importance of recreation and conversely of conservation. In a society increasingly possessed with the self, the social objectives of conservation seemed passé. But the places that conservation created, national parks close to and far from the people, became venues of leisure, places where Americans could act out their sense of their new selves, freed from the constraints of tradition, in an exhilarating environment.

In this fashion the traditional goals of conservation—preservation of nature and culture, education and enlightenment, and social uplift—fused with the individualistic aspirations of the Jazz Age. Americans flocked to their national parks in ever-growing numbers, but as many came for reasons of leisure, a cultural motif of the 1920s, as to affirm American culture. In effect, Americans gave their national parks the meaning they wanted them to have, aided by the public relations–oriented ethos of the Park Service. Mather had made his fortune in public relations and knew how to cultivate an audience. That the process took him far from what John Muir might recognize as conservation bothered him little. Reconciling the ideal with the practical, Mather recognized that a large, powerful, and loud constituency for national parks was essential if the park system was to survive—and not incidentally achieve the goals of conservation.

Thus Mather and Albright fused the goals of the national parks with the ethos of the moment in a manner that its chief competitor, the Forest Service, could not match. The Forest Service was still closely tied to the ethic of progressivism, the communal all-for-one, one-for-all spirit of the reform movement, in an age when the nation had moved on to other sensibilities. As a result the Forest Service seemed dated, a relic of a more serious and less modern era. The shift from the Forest Service's brand of utilitarian conservation to the recreation that the Park Service increasingly and sometimes inadvertently promoted illustrated not only the new role of conservation but also changes in the nation itself.

Much of conservation's traditional resource management role remained, but in the early 1920s it became tainted in no small part by government malfeasance. The Teapot Dome Scandal of 1923 brought down Secretary of the Interior Albert B. Fall. A Southwesterner devoted to the development of resources and largely devoid of scruples—he had earlier tried to create an "All-Year-Round National Park" from public domain scrublands that surrounded his ranch in southeastern New Mexico—Fall leased oil reserves at Teapot Dome, Wyoming, that were designated for the U.S. Navy to his friend, Harry F. Sinclair, of the Mammoth Oil Company, without a competitive bidding process. A second lease for Elk Hills, California, to Edward F. Doheny's Pan-American Company, drew additional attention, and Senators John Kendrick of Wyoming and Thomas J. Walsh of Montana pursued a congressional investigation. Fall resigned and was later convicted of accepting bribes related to the transaction, becoming the first cabinet member ever to go to jail, while Sinclair and Doheny were acquitted. Only President Warren G. Harding's premature death in 1923 from an embolism—called "apoplexy" at the time—saved the scandal from becoming an embarrassment to his administration.

Harding's successor, Calvin Coolidge, was as different from his predecessor as any man could be. While Harding carried on an extramarital affair throughout his adult life, Coolidge was straitlaced and colorless. He dissociated himself from Harding's administration, regaining the confidence of the public. His appointments also were far different. Hubert Work, Coolidge's first secretary of the interior, was beyond reproach. Like Coolidge himself and successors such as Dr. Ray Lyman Wilbur, who served under Herbert Hoover, Work embodied a combination of values that emphasized both the development of the West's natural resources and the idea of the greatest good for the greatest number in the long run. After Harding and the freewheeling Fall, Coolidge, Work, and their successors seemed a breath of fresh—albeit dry—air.

Talented leaders of the federal resource management agencies now won new respect. With the formidable duo of Mather and Albright at the helm, the National Park Service secured its position. The Bureau of Reclamation received a visionary leader on April 3, 1924, when Elwood Mead became its commissioner. Mead had been one of the first Americans to become involved in corporate irrigation during the 1880s and had served as state engineer (the state official in charge of water resources in Western states) in Wyoming. He brought both experience and foresight and was able to shape the new Bureau of Reclamation to the needs of the moment.

The "doctrine of prior appropriation" governed water relations in the West and Southwest. This system, which in essence meant "first in time, first in right," differed from the riparian rights granted in more humid parts of the country. In the West, ownership of land did not inherently convey the right to use water that might flow across it, which would have left the door open for consolidation of water in the hands of a few. The earliest date that any user could claim as the original time of use conferred priority over any subsequent user. Under the doctrine of prior appropriation, no one could move in upstream and divert water that people downstream were already using. The system protected people and institutions based on their use over time, a principle that, when fairly applied, essentially grandfathered in prior use. But in many cases, especially those involving Native Americans across the region and Hispanics in northern New Mexico, historic patterns of use could be legally subverted and water taken—diverted—for later arrivals. The law became a tool in the hands of leaders who sought to take from nonwhite populations the essence of their subsistence.

The larger the entity and the more water it needed, the more adept it became at consolidating water rights. More than any other city, Los Angeles excelled. Its conquest of the Owens Valley, complete by the mid-1920s, only whetted the city's thirst for more water. Los Angeles County grew from 170,000 people in 1900 to 2,785,000 in 1940, an astronomical growth rate that required consistent expansion of nearly every service. Its need for water led to larger projects, of which the Boulder Dam (now called the Hoover Dam) was first and foremost.

The long process that led to this 726-foot-high engineering marvel began more than 100 miles down the Colorado River from Black Canyon, where the dam was eventually built. In the Mojave Desert, which averages about 2.4 inches of rainfall per year, a man named Charles Rockwood recruited the most famous private irrigationist of his day, George Chaffey, and in 1901 the two cut a diversion channel to bring water from the river into an area then called the Valley of the Dead. Rockwood renamed it the Imperial Valley, and within one year the area boasted two towns, 2,000 settlers, and 100,000 acres of crops. The Imperial Valley seemed a reclamation paradise, one of those places where the ingenuity of human beings could transcend the obvious limits of nature.

The turn of the twentieth century inaugurated an exceptionally wet thirty-year period in much of the West. In some places people built unrealistic expectations of land use; in others, hopes and dreams were washed away under a cavalcade of water. By 1904 Chaffey and Rockwood's original diversion had silted up as had a second, temporary channel built while the first one was being cleaned. When spring floods came early, the temporary ditch could not hold the water, and the river ripped into the irrigated land with fury. The water cut into the loamy Imperial Valley soil at the rate of one foot per second, creating the eerie apparition of twenty-foot-high waterfalls marching backward toward the original channel. Homes were swept away, fields drowned beneath the water, and people of the region came to watch the strange wall of water moving backward at a slow crawl.

The fields of the Imperial Valley were not the only casualty of the water. Edward H. Harriman's Southern Pacific Railroad had built a spur to the region; rather than give up the rails, Harriman bought Rockwood's defunct irrigation company and tried to achieve what the irrigationists could not. From 1905 to 1907, three of the wettest years ever in the Colorado Basin, Harriman's trains carried rock and gravel to plug the breach in the channel. Each time the water washed away their efforts. Finally in 1907 the repairs held, and the Colorado River appeared to be tamed—at least for a while.

The waves of destructive floods left an imprint on the minds of people downstream. They recognized that there was only one way to secure the region, allow it to grow unimpeded, and protect crops and people from destructive nature: a dam had to be built upstream that could regulate the flow of the Colorado River. These objectives of the Imperial Valley residents dovetailed nicely with those of the city of Los Angeles, already well on its way to outstripping the water supply it took from the Owens Valley. In order to continue adding population, California needed water. The logical source was the Colorado River. Two different kinds of development in the most populous and increasingly the most powerful state in the West joined forces in support of a dam.

But opposition by upper basin states blocked California's monopolization of water. The upper basin states rightly regarded California's water grab as the death knell for their own development aspirations. After more than a decade of delay, opponents of the dam were undone by a court case. In 1922 the U.S. Supreme Court, in *Wyoming v. California*, held that states that used the prior appropriation doctrine in internal water allocation, as did all the basin states, were also bound by it in interstate disputes if they shared a common water source. This gave the water in the Colorado River to California at the expense of the other river states.

Legislation to establish the dam, the Swing-Johnson Bill, sent chills through the rest of the intermountain West and prompted the Colorado River Compact, an agreement between Western states that adjudicated water distribution in the Colorado River and was designed to fairly divide the water. Faced with the court decision and the dam bill, the upper basin states were forced to sue for peace.

The distribution of water under the Colorado River Compact was farcical at best and ludicrous at worst. The Reclamation Service estimated that the Colorado River contained 17.5 million acre-feet of water. (An acre foot was the standard measure; it denoted the amount of water needed to cover one acre of land with one foot of water.) The Colorado may have held that much water at a given moment during one of the very wet years in the early 1900s, but its annual flow in an average year was closer to 12 million acre-feet. The compact divided the river's drainage into two basins, using Lee's Ferry, Arizona, just south of the Utah state line, as the boundary. The lower basin states—California, Arizona, and Nevada, with portions of New Mexico—received 7.5 million acre feet; the upper basin states—Colorado, Wyoming, and Utah, which together produced more than 70 percent of the water in the river, and most of New Mexico—received an equal amount. Each basin was to divide its water among its own states as it wished. Mexico received 1.5 million acre-feet from the fictitious allotment, and the remaining 1 million acre-feet went to the lower basin as a sort of bonus for agreeing to negotiate at all. In the aftermath of *Wyoming v. California*, the lower basin states had felt vulnerable to preemption by California.

Although the delegates could agree, their states did not accept the compact. After signing it in November 1922, the delegates took the compact home for ratification, only to find it an extremely unpopular piece of legislation. No one liked it; every constituency felt shortchanged, and the agreement was pilloried in the press and in statehouses across the West. After six years there was no resolution. In 1928 Congress finally intervened. It authorized the Boulder Dam and the All-American Canal for the Imperial Valley and limited California's share of water from the compact to 4.4 million acre-feet on the condition that six of the seven compact states ratify the agreement. With Nevada's 300,000 acre-feet and California's 4.4 million, Arizona received 2.8 million acre-feet, less than it wanted. As a result, while the other six states ratified the compact, Arizona refused. With the congressional requirement that only six of seven need approve the compact, Arizona's refusal was meaningless in the short term. The stage was set for Western growth, with federally funded dams regulating water apportioned by the principal of "might makes right." As early as 1929, when construction on Boulder Dam began, the axiom "in the American West, water flows uphill to money" was entirely true.

The construction of Boulder Dam catapulted the Bureau of Reclamation to a position of prominence near that of the U.S. Army Corps of Engineers, the federal agency most responsible

for the modification of the American landscape in the twentieth century. Beginning with the Ohio and Mississippi naviga-
tion improvement acts of 1824, the Corps had begun an
aggressive civil works program aimed at controlling the nation's natural resources. Its projects ranged from the construction of federal buildings and monuments in Washington,
D.C., to the building of the National Road facilitating westward expansion and an extensive system of military forts and
installations to protect that expansion. Its grandest accom-
plishment was the building of the Panama Canal, one of the
greatest engineering feats in history. After false starts on a
canal by the French in the late 1800s, which led many to believe the project impossible, Americans took it over. Under
the watchful eye of President Theodore Roosevelt, the Corps
succeeded in rapidly completing the Culebra Cut, the most
difficult section of the canal. When completed, the Panama
Canal seemed to confirm that humans, and Americans in particular, were capable of reordering nature to suit their needs.

It was no coincidence that the office of the U.S. government
responsible for environmental engineering until the 1930s was
a branch of the military. For most of America's history, the
modification of nature had been approached like a war. The
massive environmental engineering projects of the Corps
demonstrated the American faith that human ingenuity and
brute force could impose order on chaotic nature. This faith
was put to the ultimate test in the Corps' attempts to control
the destructive annual flooding of the Mississippi River with
an extensive system of levees, dams, and spillways.

Following the successful construction of the Panama Canal,
the effort to tame the mighty Mississippi occupied the genius
and hubris of the Corps of Engineers. Yearly floods had always ravaged the Mississippi Delta, displaced residents, destroyed crops and property, and caused general economic
havoc. Catastrophic floods in 1912, 1913, and especially 1927,

when flood waters claimed 16 million acres and at least 250 lives, turned national attention on the river and generated support for a comprehensive federal effort to bring it under control. In the decades after the devastating flood of 1927, the Corps constructed an extensive series of levees and spillways to protect people and property along the river from the Midwest to the Gulf of Mexico.

Boulder Dam served as the prototype for the New Deal development projects of the 1930s. When Herbert Hoover was sworn in as president in 1929, some observers considered him the best-qualified man ever to assume the presidency. But Hoover's personal philosophy of self-help and his devotion to laissez-faire capitalism prevented him from engineering a broad-based response to the depression that began after the stock market crash. As unemployment rose, families crumbled, and people starved, Hoover and his cabinet played medicine ball on the White House lawn to show their physical—and presumably psychological—fitness to deal with the crisis. In deep distress and genuine pain, the public rejected Hoover's efforts and his attempts to assuage their fears by voting him out of office in the 1932 election.

The new president, Franklin D. Roosevelt, brought a different set of ideas to Washington. Embracing the concepts of the British economist John Maynard Keynes, Roosevelt and his Brains Trust, as the group of his closest advisers was labeled, fashioned a widespread spending program designed to "prime the pump" of the national economy. Since Roosevelt was willing to engage in deficit spending to promote economic recovery, and because federal lands throughout the nation—including national parks and forests and other public lands—required work, a fusion occurred of the social goals of conservation and the economic goals of the New Deal.

Roosevelt's interest in conservation was a result of his class background and his personal inclinations. He enjoyed a privileged upbringing at Hyde Park, New York, that taught him the principles of turn-of-the-century conservation; until he was stricken with polio in the early 1920s, the new president had been an avid outdoorsman. Like his cousin Theodore, FDR envisioned himself a steward of land. Elected to the New York state legislature in 1911, he gravitated to conservation issues. As chairman of the legislature's Forest, Fish, and Game Committee, he introduced eight separate bills to regulate hunting and fishing. Limiting resource use was a solution that reflected his class background. The people at whom he directed such legislation typically were subsistence hunters and fishermen or commercial outfits. Their goals and those of the conservation establishment conflicted, and during the Progressive era, law typically sided with the most powerful.

Roosevelt faced a complicated situation in conservation when he came to the White House. He was a Democrat elected by a landslide, but conservation had become the province of the Republican party. During the 1920s the leaders of most conservation organizations felt their affiliation with business interests to be more important than the political objectives they had inherited from the Progressive era. Partly it was the tenor of the time, an era of rising spirits, and partly the class background of the individuals who rose to conservation leadership. The American Forestry Association, once a professional group of conservationists and foresters, became dominated by timber concerns. Industry lobbying groups supplied most of its funding, and the organization's leaders, Ovid M. Butler and George Dupont Pratt, were conservative Republicans with close ties to the industry. Elsewhere Republicans headed the Audubon Association, More Game Birds, the National Parks Association, the American Museum of Natural History, and the American Planning and Civic Association, among others. Conservation had become a part of business instead of an indicator of political outlook, a partisan position mostly for Republicans rather than a bipartisan consensus.

One of the ways the new president crossed this bridge and brought conservation into his fold was by recruiting Republicans to his administration. Roosevelt's appointees to the two federal agencies with the greatest potential for conservation work were both Republicans—defectors from their party but long-standing members of the GOP nonetheless. Harold L. Ickes became secretary of the interior, and Henry A. Wallace, who had already left the Republican party, accepted the position of secretary of agriculture. Both men had abandoned Hoover for Roosevelt in 1932. Ickes led a group of liberal Republicans into the Democratic fold, for he found in Roosevelt, he said, a leader whose conservation interests matched his own. Roosevelt's conservation goals paralleled those of the Republican leaders of the conservation movement, blurring the political boundary for avid supporters of conservation. The new president ranked the human use of nature first, cared for wildlife second, and placed preservation last. This hierarchy of views coincided with those of Republicans of the president's class who were interested in conservation, and among them Roosevelt found considerable support.

FDR's conservation programs fused his goals for the outdoors with his objectives for the nation. The two most prominent, the Civilian Conservation Corps (CCC), essentially a military-style program that put young men to work on federal lands throughout the country, and the Tennessee Valley Authority (TVA), were central to the New Deal. Both were comprehensive programs that put people to work and created opportunities in their wake. Both served conservation goals in the turn-of-the-century sense, and both fulfilled the pressing objectives of the New Deal. Roosevelt's agenda and the needs of the country nicely dovetailed, making the New Deal's conservation initiatives the most impressive federal conservation program undertaken to that time.

The CCC, one of Roosevelt's first ideas after he took office, was a focal point. A few weeks into the presidency, FDR proposed that unemployed young men be sent into rural areas of the nation to perform basic work on federal and state lands. They would work in forestry, prevent soil erosion, and help with flood-control projects. As it developed, the CCC became one of the ways in which the government put people to work and helped them see a positive future in otherwise dismal economic times. The CCC took single men between the ages of eighteen and twenty-five and gave them hard physical work in the nation's forests, parks, and public lands.

CCC workers were counted among the fortunate during the depression. The young men lived in military-style barracks, worked six days a week for a dollar a day (all but five dollars was sent home to their families each month), and built roads, trails, firebreaks, structures, and a range of other necessities and amenities on public lands. Much of the work was necessary—although the earthen dam constructed in western Kansas that silted over from the blowing dirt of the Dust Bowl just as it was completed stands out as a visible exception—and all of it, even the earthen dam, put thousands of men to work and funneled money to destitute communities. During its nine-year existence, more than 2 million enrollees worked in 198 CCC camps in national park areas and 697 camps in state, county, and municipal parks alone. The national forests and other public lands contained countless others. Under the various bureaus that administered CCC programs—the Emergency Conservation Work program (ECW), the Public Works Administration (PWA), the Works Progress Administration (WPA), and others—more than 1,000 miles of park roads and 249 miles of parkways were built in national park areas.

When it was completed in the late 1930s, the Tennessee Valley Authority was the largest and most comprehensive regional planning effort ever attempted in the United States. The passage of the TVA act set up a government corporation to develop the resources of the Tennessee River. The forty thousand square miles it drained were among the most poverty-stricken and least developed in the nation; in the 1930s much of the area did not yet have electricity. The river itself was uncontrollable. It raged in wet seasons, washing away topsoil and flooding lowlands. In dry seasons it became a mere trickle, useless to the people who depended on it. The region's problems seemed chronic and unsolvable: floods, fierce soil erosion, a preindustrial economy, and little opportunity.

TVA presented an opportunity to redefine an entire region, a project of a scope and scale never before attempted by government in the United States. It would create economic opportunity for the downtrodden by taking a wild environment and controlling it for long-term human advantage. The goals of the project paralleled those of earlier conservation leaders such as Gifford Pinchot. TVA took an untamed river system—at Muscle Shoals, Alabama, the Tennessee River dropped 137 feet in 37 miles—and converted it to human use, following the principle of the greatest good for the greatest number in the long run. Muscle Shoals had long been recognized as a valuable dam site. The TVA dam built there, and the forty-one others in the project, were state-of-the-art developments. They produced enormous amounts of cheap electricity, bringing much of the region into the twentieth century. TVA also established flood control for the region and made the Tennessee River navigable.

TVA's primary purpose was to improve the lives of the 3.5 million people who lived in its vicinity. Appalachia had long been among the poorest parts of the nation, and life there remained difficult. By providing the primary energy source of modernity and teaching the techniques of modern farming, TVA expected to begin to rectify the long history of privation in the region. Roosevelt himself announced that "TVA is primarily intended to change and improve the standards of living" of Tennessee Valley residents. It was a noble goal in the 1930s, an experiment on a grand and magnificent scale, even if its results were not always as grand as its aspirations.

Agencies such as the Corps of Engineers also benefited from the New Deal. The 1936 Flood Control Act made the Corps responsible for flood control for the entire nation and united its efforts with the New Deal public works mission. State-spanning levees seemed finally to bring the Mississippi River under control and encouraged a new confidence which brought unprecedented growth into areas prone to flooding and gave the Corps a position to claim its piece of the New Deal pie. The Bonneville Dam on the Columbia River in Washington State was one of many Corps projects during the Roosevelt years. Its construction testified both to the shared mission of the New Deal bureaucratic structure and the overlapping missions and constituencies of the Corps of Engineers and the Bureau of Reclamation.

Elsewhere environmental calamity coincided with economic disaster to cause one of the largest internal migrations in American history. Agriculture on the Great Plains had grown enormously since the late nineteenth century, spurred by technological advance and an unusually wet period that stretched roughly from 1900 until the late 1920s. Mechanization made it possible for farmers to plant and harvest far greater acreage than they could behind a plow, and the abundance of rainfall allowed people to grow crops in places that otherwise could not sustain agriculture. Between 1879 and 1929, lands under cultivation on the plains increased tenfold. Most of the 103 million acres in cultivation on the plains in

1929, up from 12 million in 1879, were semi-arid marginal land that bore crops only because of the era's unusual moisture.

Until the early 1920s this great expansion paralleled the robust American economy. Agriculture had been a stepchild of America's industrialization, leading first to dissatisfaction among farmers and then to the agrarian rebellion and its political arm, populism, at the end of the nineteenth century. Although prosperity returned to agriculture in 1909, World War I enshrined it. Beginning in August 1914 with the decline in European harvests, American grain became the dominant commodity on the world market. Prices rose to levels beyond the wildest imagination of farmers and encouraged them to plant still more. After the war, American crops remained alone in the world market until the early 1920s, when European fields again produced sufficient quantities for the market. The glut then drove crop prices down, bankrupting cotton producers such as Texan Sam Johnson, the father of Lyndon B. Johnson, and trapping countless others who had borrowed money to buy land or equipment. American farmers responded by producing even greater commodities, driving prices down throughout the decade. Each time prices dropped, farmers produced more—as if the problems of excess could be solved by growing ever more. By the late 1920s Great Plains farmers produced more than they ever had but earned roughly the same income they had enjoyed at the beginning of the decade.

As long as rains continued and the economy expanded, the scenario held. But in 1929 the two pillars of this faux prosperity toppled together. Not only did the stock market crash, but on the Great Plains the rains stopped. A drought began that first slowed agricultural expansion, then halted it altogether. In 1931 Montana and the Dakotas were as arid as the Sonoran Desert of northern Mexico. By early 1934 some parts of the plains had not seen rain in more than two years. On May 9–10 that year, the drought burst onto the national consciousness when dust from the plains blackened skies throughout the nation. Huge clouds of blowing dirt, looking much like tornadoes, came swirling from the west, sending 350 million tons of sand and dirt on the wind toward urban America. The dirt was everywhere: it filtered through cracks in the sides of houses, under doors, into food being prepared, and even into car engines. A fine film of dirt covered everything. Drifts of dirt rose against the sides of houses and buildings. The taste of dust in the air was ubiquitous. Its presence confirmed that the drought was real. The assets of hundreds of thousands of people—the soil from which they scraped their living—was blowing away in the jetstream.

And it traveled far. The red dirt of Oklahoma could be found on the island of Bermuda, 700 miles off the eastern seaboard, and on the decks of ships in the Atlantic Ocean. Midday on May 10 in Buffalo, New York, was as dark as night. Schenectady, New York, about 150 miles up the Hudson River from New York City, was inundated with blowing dirt. Throughout Texas, in the typically humid South, along the Ohio River, the blowing dirt from the Great Plains signaled ecological catastrophe. A pattern of storms continued until the end of the decade. Beginning in 1935, no year recorded fewer than 40 plains dust storms that cut visibility to less than one mile. In 1937, the worst year, 72 such storms occurred. On April 14, 1935, the worst of the dust storms hit. In the region the day was ever after called Black Sunday. Observing from the outside, a reporter labeled the region the Dust Bowl. The name stuck.

For the people of the Great Plains, many of whom were poor farmers on marginal land, the Dust Bowl served as an incentive to leave. As the dust blew, the region turned to desert. Fields that had once sustained crops became sand; furrows

that had once held seed looked like something children created with a pail and shovel at the beach. For many farmers, so
close to subsistence to begin with, the calamity was more than
they could bear. It forced them off the land. They packed up
in countless contraptions and headed for the golden land of
California, where they believed that fruit grew everywhere
and was there for the picking. As it turned out, most of the
picking these "Okies" did was in fields owned by large grow-
ers, who paid poor wages and offered abysmal living conditions. The predicament of the Joad family in John Steinbeck's
Grapes of Wrath typified their experience. In the novel Steinbeck attributed their situation not to the Dust Bowl but to the
spread of corporate farming in northeastern Oklahoma. Despite the different reason behind their move west, the Joads
have come to represent the Dust Bowl and its victims in the
American consciousness.

The Dust Bowl destroyed the regional agricultural economy and considerably diminished the population of the
Southern plains. In Haskell County, Kansas, near the heart of
the Dust Bowl, the county's population fell from 2,804 in 1930
to 2,465 in 1935, and further still in 1940 to 2,100. This one-
quarter depopulation typified the region, suggesting that not
only farmers were affected but also the residents of regional
communities. In Sublette, Kansas, the 1930 population was
673; by 1940 it had fallen to 582. In nearby Satanta, 508 made
their homes in 1930; a decade later the number had fallen to
345. The decline of communities hurt social institutions—
churches closed, clubs folded, towns disappeared. The toll of
the Dust Bowl was far more than merely economic.

Under the New Deal, the federal government took the lead
in responding to such disasters. The Soil Conservation Service, a typical New Deal agency, sent its operatives into the
field to attempt to recreate ground cover from which agriculture could follow. Where these conservation agronomists, as

the SCS's representatives were labeled, found sand dunes they strove to create first grass and later crops. In some cases they were successful, but even when recovery was harder to come by, the presence of the SCS offered a ray of hope against the dark background of dust-clouded skies. Their impact was so profound that some residents likened them to the cavalry of the Old West, whose troopers arrived at the last possible moment to rescue individuals and communities in distress. Between 1937 and 1942 in the Amarillo, Texas, area, SCS sponsored the reclamation of nearly one million acres of damaged land. SCS representatives taught new techniques and planted shelterbelts of trees to divide fields and help keep topsoil in place (one of the consequences of the great agricultural expansion of the early 1900s was the destruction of ground cover, trees, and shrubs that stood in the way of cultivation). The SCS engaged in an entire range of activities that mirrored both the relief and self-help programs of the New Deal and the foreign aid shipments that followed World War II.

By December 1941, when the Japanese attacked Pearl Harbor and the United States entered World War II, the efforts of the SCS had stabilized much of the Dust Bowl area. Although the region was different now, both in its demography and its ecology, it had recovered as at least a partially viable economic region. In the end the federal government could claim a victory over nature in the Dust Bowl, even if the solution never addressed the root causes of the tragedy—the fundamentally American idea that more is better and that the route to abundance travels through technological transformation of the landscape.

The dawn of World War II changed the climate for conservationists. The social objectives of the New Deal were set aside in the urgency of preparedness, and conservation fell from the table of priorities. Factories that had often been idle during

the depression now sprang to life, especially on the West Coast
and in Midwestern cities, to create the materials necessary to
wage global war. The increase in industrial activity across the
country—from California to New England—had dire consequences in some locales. In Cleveland the Cuyahoga River
that ran through the city was so loaded with industrial wastes
and toxic materials that it caught on fire. Los Angeles experienced its first real smog. Waterways around the nation were
fouled with waste, and skies clouded with emissions.

In the context of the war, conservation lost its claims to a
central position in national policy. The war threatened the
survival of the nation; conservation would have to wait. While
Americans revered their outdoors, it had more important uses
during the war: raw materials were needed to stock the arsenal of democracy. Conservation had a soft underbelly: it was a
full-stomach issue, one important to people largely in good
times or when it could be harnessed to the needs of difficult
economic times. The war challenged its goals and placed its issues on the back burner.

The war also opened the next door in human endeavor, the
Pandora's Box that ever after vexed the United States and the
world. The threat of Nazi science pushed the United States
into new areas of research with vast but—at the time—largely
unrecognized consequences for the human species. From the
beginning of the Atomic Age—the moment that Italian expa-
triate scientist Enrico Fermi manipulated control rods of the
first exponential pile of uranium and graphite under the
stands of Stagg Field on the University of Chicago campus in
December 1942—science opened a new world, constructed
from the basic building blocks of the universe. It was a race
against the enemy to harness the power of the atom. Once that
power was released, nothing was ever again the same.

Science became a wartime tool. Supported by the investment of vast amounts of federal money, the research drive to-

ward an atomic bomb continued at the Trinity Site in southern New Mexico, where the first atomic device was tested on July 16, 1945. The predawn blast broke windows more than three hundred miles away and created a new material—sand turned into a form of glass called "trinitite," after the location where the blast took place. Because of the bright flash that accompanied the mushroom cloud of the blast, July 16, 1945, became known as the day the sun rose twice. Less than a month later, the power of the atom became a weapon. Atomic bombs were dropped first on Hiroshima, a Japanese city with some military significance. At least eighty thousand died, but when the Japanese failed to surrender, a second bomb was dropped a few days later on Nagasaki. Some scientists were astonished at how well their experiment worked; others expressed shock that the world did not go up in flames, for they expected that an atomic explosion would ignite the earth's atmosphere. Like the public, scientists responded with a combination of exhilaration about the surrender of the Japanese and horror at how victory had finally been achieved.

It was a fitting conundrum, this expression of America's faith in science and technology and revulsion at its power. The atomic bomb was more powerful than anything the world had ever seen. It changed the parameters of human endeavor and required new and different means of individuals and nations to ensure that the use of atomic weapons did not become a standard of warfare. Atomic fission was more than another toy. It required a rethinking of the fundamental way in which humans did their business.

The opening of the Atomic Age added one more piece of evidence that traditional conservation had become obsolete. While John Muir, Gifford Pinchot, and Harold L. Ickes had dealt with the most crucial issues of their moment, the interest in mountaintops, wild playgrounds, and the conservation of natural resources now ceased to define the boundaries of the problem for most Americans. Living in cities where the air was fouled by smokestack emissions and the rivers were ugly with effluent, and threatened by the prospect of imminent destruction, Americans grappled with more practically serious issues. To retain its viability, conservation needed to change.

4

The Democratization of Conservation

IN THE AFTERMATH of World War II, interest in conservation remained confined to a narrow realm of American society. With the primacy of groups such as the Sierra Club, the Izaak Walton League, and the Wilderness Society, what had begun with elites and spread to a wide portion of the middle class now returned to its narrowest origins. In 1945 conservation's advocates represented only one class of Americans, a group that could best be described as the privileged. Their interests were limited to species preservation and the protection of existing wilderness. Few if any of them were interested in the effects of the spreading suburbs, questions of equal access to federal land for development or recreational purposes, industrial and auto emissions, and related issues. Conservation groups tended to ally closely with federal land management agencies and mimic agency perspective on issues. For such agencies, often declining in power in a nation transformed by war, the advocates of conservation served as a valuable and usually docile ally.

The postwar era was characterized by a number of trends that democratized attitudes about conservation. The pent-up demand for auto travel and increasing affluence after the war propelled millions of Americans to see their national parks and forests. As more of them vacationed, exemplified by record numbers of visitors at Grand Canyon National Park each month after August 1945, they had an impact on the natural world that soon caused them to take notice. What Americans found in many of their national parks and forests shocked them: decrepit and outdated campgrounds, garbage piled high, and a lack of facilities and staff to manage them. The growth of Western cities as a result of the war brought millions more people in close proximity to the most stunning attributes of American nature, and their demands for electricity, water, homes, and roads made a visible dent in forests and crowded the banks of rivers, lakes, and oceans. Clear-cutting of forests adjacent to highways in particular inspired public ire. Still convinced of the efficacy of technological solutions to all kinds of problems, Americans began to recognize that their actions in the physical world, multiplied by their ever-increasing numbers, foretold dire consequences for the land that made the nation special.

But what to do about it? When Americans looked at their parks and forests and saw a mess, they could turn to no politically viable organizations that addressed the problem. The situation recalled the turn of the century, before Theodore Roosevelt became president and when the various currents of reform stood alone and discrete. At mid-century ordinary Americans looked at the direction of their society with a combination of awe and trepidation, and found nowhere to express the force of their dissatisfaction. Something or someone was needed to galvanize the public and create a forum in which to express the disquiet of postwar society.

The proposed Colorado River Storage Program (CRSP) provided the spark that ignited the postwar conservation movement. A plan to build a series of dams along the Colorado River to provide hydroelectric power to growing Western cities, and to support the activities of the Atomic Energy Commission in Nevada and Utah, the CRSP included a dam that would flood Dinosaur National Monument in northwest

Colorado and northeast Utah. To the largely apolitical conservation groups of the mid-century, this seemed a reprise of the Hetch-Hetchy battle of the early 1900s, and they set out to stop the project known as Echo Park Dam. By developing a wider public constituency than ever before, they forced an end to one part of the project, in the process acquiescing to the construction of the other dams envisioned by the Bureau of Reclamation. One of these, the Glen Canyon Dam, inundated a vast area memorialized in photographer Eliot Porter's classic book *The Place No One Knew*. This seminal conservation work alerted the public that lands outside of national parks possessed qualities as special as those within designated boundaries.

The Echo Park controversy was a throwback to the Progressive era. Orchestrated by groups with roots in the turn-of-the-century conservation movement but transformed by the very nature of their attempt to slow progress, the struggle to save Dinosaur National Monument ended an era in conservation, a phase that could rightly be called the gentleman's club. Future efforts became more broadly based and, as a result, not as well organized and controlled and more diverse in sentiment. Conservation changed its stripes. It represented a greater number of voices in American society—though at times the sounds that emerged were more cacophonous than harmonious.

At the end of World War II, conservation had lost much of the stature it had gained earlier in the century and was on the way to becoming a nonissue in American society. Its ideas seemed rooted in an earlier time, in an age when progress was merely possible, not essential. World War II revolutionized the nation; in its aftermath came an economic, social, and geographic expansion that transformed American life. It improved for nearly everybody. Many of those who migrated to cities to work in defense-related industries found that they liked their new urban lives better than their poverty-stricken prewar experience on the farm. The range of opportunities and the excitement of urban living had great appeal, especially in contrast to the narrow horizons of rural life. African Americans found historic barriers starting to crack. Beginning with President Harry S Truman's 1946 appointment of a Committee on Civil Rights and continuing with the appearance of Jackie Robinson in a Brooklyn Dodgers uniform, a tortuous process began to define a new and more inclusive society. Robinson and the handful of ballplayers who followed him were symbols of the ways that the nation was becoming different. In conservation, the focus shifted from the placid and largely elitist outlook of the prewar era.

The war helped create the context in which African Americans could lobby for their civil rights and receive a hearing from the public at large. Women tasted a delicious new freedom during the war, and though many returned to the home or to lower-paying, lower-status jobs after their stints in the defense industry ended, all the "Rosie the Riveters" (as the women in the wartime industrial workplace were labeled) allowed a generation of American women to stake their claim to social equality. The walls of the pink ghettos of teaching and nursing began to crumble, at first ever so slowly, then with an accelerating speed that stunned those who believed in the old order. The global battle for "freedom" of peoples, ethnic groups, and nation states waged in World War II became a catalyst of the individual rights revolution in the United States. Those who had regarded the fight against fascism as their cause fought for the rights of strangers across the seas. Their children learned to embrace individual rights above social goals. After the war, people worked longer hours, had more spending money, and enjoyed more ways to spend it. New institutions such as drive-in restaurants fit the needs of the time, reflecting the emphasis on speed that characterized the postwar world. Americans wanted more and they wanted it faster. Success in the postwar era depended on remembering this axiom. After World War II, Americans pieced together a new and different society that made conservation, as it had been practiced since the early twentieth century, obsolete.

Urban and rural areas of the nation also developed with surprising speed. Cities expanded, grafting on new suburbs filled with single-family houses along ribbons of road that extended farther and farther from urban cores. The most famous such community, Levittown on Long Island outside New York City, began a boom that took the nation from 114,000 new housing starts in 1944 to 1,183,000 in 1948. In 1950 construction began on nearly 1.7 million new single-family homes, many like the original Levittown homes: 720- to 1,200-square-foot units with two bedrooms and one bath on a concrete slab, built in the Cape Cod style. Such homes did not provide a great deal of space, but it was more than most American families had ever known. They also accentuated American individualism, the sense that a person's home was truly his castle, where he needed to consult no one outside the family about his decisions.

The development of Levittown foreshadowed urban growth in postwar America. Even American law favored single-family housing, with the result that the urban center of most cities began to be transformed from space used in multiple ways by many kinds of people to space used in fewer ways by fewer, increasingly poor and immigrant classes. Beginning in 1950 and continuing for more than thirty years, most of the nation's largest cities lost population to the suburbs that surrounded them. By 1970 more Americans lived in suburbs than in cities, connected to their work by a grid of freeways, divided highways, and four-lane roads. Named Redmond, Metairie, Turlock, Tarzana, Overland Park, and Buffalo

Grove, suburbs abounded. They created a world of their own. Farms, ranches, and open space had all been transformed into urban space; automobiles and their passengers came to places that only recently had been so far off the beaten path that they did not appear on maps. The first impact of postwar prosperity took place on the lands that became the roads, homes, stores, and shopping centers of a new, polyglot American culture: the suburbs.

An unparalleled economic boom raised almost everyone's sights. Military service provided veterans with unequaled benefits—government loans to finance housing, funds to support an education, and other mechanisms that offered remarkable opportunities to people who before the war had expected to scrape for everything they would ever get. In an expanding economy, utilizing more and more natural resources, everyone seemed to have a chance. After the war, Americans of every race believed they had earned the right to live better. Their sacrifices overseas and on the home front were their proof, and the prize most men and women wanted was a wider variety of better consumer goods. Industry responded with more and better of everything. "New and improved" became a cliché as Americans crowded the marketplace to sample the wares of industrial society. Cars, washing machines, refrigerators, and other "big ticket" items disappeared from stores as fast as the nation could produce them. Americans consumed, for a while blissfully unaware of the environmental cost of that consumption.

Rapid economic growth had a visible downside for Americans, measured in the declining quality of air and water as well as in the marring of the American landscape. Wartime expansion of industrialization had accelerated the spread of heavy industry. Airplane construction, shipbuilding, and the mining and processing of minerals created industrial prosperity in remote places. The war brought the benefits and consequences of industrialization to places that had little previous experience with it.

All of these endeavors involved severe environmental consequences made worse by ignorance of the impact of chemical and industrial processes on people, land, and water. The most dramatic example of the problem began a few days before Halloween, 1948. A thermal inversion blanketed the Northeast and Midwest, trapping industrial by-products and emissions between the ground and the low layers of heavy fog. Pilots could not see clearly enough to take commercial airliners into the air, and airports backed up with irate travelers. Poor visibility impeded even automobile traffic, leaving long lines of cars with frustrated drivers creeping toward their destinations. People with respiratory ailments or even minor breathing problems flocked to hospitals. A sticky film of muck, the price of industrial prosperity, coated the region, causing some to ask if prosperity was worth the price.

About thirty miles down the Monongahela River from Pittsburgh stood the industrial cities of Donora and Webster, Pennsylvania. Located near a zinc smelting plant, the two towns typified the condition of industrial America. Even on the most ordinary of days, smoke from the zinc smelter was "acrid and poisonous, it penetrated everywhere," wrote local author Thomas Bell in his classic study of the steel industry, *Out of This Furnace*, "making automobile headlights necessary in Webster's streets, setting the river-boat pilots to cursing God, and destroying every living thing on the hills." Here, in places with plenty of experience with the consequences of progress and wholly dependent on industry, the inversion turned deadly. Seventeen people died in a twelve-hour period, and thousands more gasped for air. The "mysterious death-dealing smog," as the *Pittsburgh Post-Gazette* called it, came not from airborne effluent from the smokestacks of the local zinc works but from the accumulation of ordinary smoke trapped beneath the inversion layer. Newspaper columnist Walter Winchell broadcast news of the tragedy on his nationally syndicated radio program, and on Sunday, Halloween morning, United States Steel ordered its zinc smelter shut down. A powerful midday rain dispersed the smog, but when the air cleared the damage was real: twenty people had died of asphyxiation and more than six hundred were hospitalized—in a population of about fourteen thousand. In the wrong circumstances, the price of prosperity could be deadly.

Donora was an exceptional case but one that spoke clearly to the circumstances of postwar society. World War II changed the nation in countless ways, but in no single way with more lasting impact than in its sources of energy. Before the war, coal powered the United States; oil was significant but hardly dominant. Pipelines and refineries, however, were integral components of wartime industrial expansion, and after the war refined oil products became the dominant source of fuel on the planet. Oil was easier to transport and store than coal, and it contained more energy per unit of volume. Beginning in 1949, oil began an ascent that took its consumption in the United States from 5.8 billion barrels that year to more than 16.4 billion in 1971. General Motors Corporation fueled this process and became the bellwether American business. It made so many more cars than all its competitors combined, and amassed so much power and influence, that few disputed the oft-repeated slogan, "What's good for General Motors is good for the country." Powered by cheap imported gasoline, automobiles dominated the landscape and became the preeminent symbol of success in the United States.

This optimistic extravagance had consequences that were easy to miss. The cars of the late 1940s and 1950s looked gorgeous—sleek, long, and finned—but they burned gasoline extravagantly, packed the roads, and left a haze in the atmosphere with their exhaust fumes. The gasoline contained lead, recognized even in ancient Rome for its destructive effects on humans exposed to it. At rush hour, crowded corners reeked of automobile emissions; the smell of fuel and an invisible coating of lead particulate were everywhere. Cities such as Los Angeles endured a new hazard, something called "smog" (a derivation of the words *smoke* and *fog*), which described filthy, thick, greyish air that resulted from smokestacks and auto emissions and spoiled the scenic vistas of southern California. The prevailing high-pressure conditions that produced so much cloudless sunshine also made temperature inversions common, trapping cooler air closer to the surface and disseminating hotter emissions widely across the Los Angeles basin. In its first encounter with an inversion seeded with industrial emissions in 1943, Los Angeles endured four hours of noxious misery, a by-product of wartime industrial development. By 1948 the city had established an Air Pollution District, and by the mid-1950s smog had become a symbol of Los Angeles, remarked upon in the national press and by weathermen who sometimes described the air as "neurotic." The Golden State and the California Dream, the postwar American myth of success, had been tarnished. Smog illustrated what was perilous about the rush to southern California—and not incidentally what was wrong with postwar progress in the United States.

Smog did not routinely kill, as did the inversion layer in Donora, Pennsylvania. It was far more benign, a daily low-level annoyance, an inescapable reminder of the cost of urban prosperity. "Driving out of Los Angeles," novelist John Rechy wrote, "I looked in my rearview mirror . . . And I saw reflected a gray amorphous 'dome,' a cloud created by entrapped smoke and lingering fog enclosing the 'city of lost angels,' the city of daily apocalypse." Like Los Angeles and the automobiles of the time, the surface of American society seemed sleek and beautiful, expansive and risk-free, but post-war industrial progress included real discontents.

Despite such obvious signs as smog, the environmental consequences of progress were easy to ignore. Europe and the world waited to be rebuilt, and American technology supplied the impetus. Economic prosperity seemed within reach of a larger and more diverse segment of the population than ever before, and with fuel abundant, opportunity widely available, and people focusing on personal rather than collective problems, few paid attention to sooty skies, fouled river basins and lakes, and the increasingly grimy feel of industrial cities. From the point of view of millions of ordinary Americans, the technological revolution brought impressive benefits. As they drove their elegant cars to work in the expanded industrial economy, to steel mills, chemical plants, aerospace and weapons facilities, and the numerous other enterprises transformed as a result of wartime innovation, they assumed that their work contained no untoward risk. For "Hydrocarbon Man," author Daniel Yergin's term for the workers who derived a higher standard of living from the rise of petroleum and its by-products, risks were considered an integral component of progress.

Even critics of American society in the 1950s and early 1960s ignored growing evidence that progress threatened the quality of life. Daniel Bell, David Riesman, Betty Friedan, and William H. Whyte challenged the organization and values of contemporary society, but only from a social perspective. They never questioned the physical world's ability to support more people, industries, houses, and cars. When they criticized industrial society, they showed how a rigid, hierarchical society affected individuals, not how human action risked the planet. During the 1950s the problems of people, not the physical environment or the implications of human actions for the long-term survival of the species, dominated public discourse.

The leaders of the conservation movement willingly joined in the laudatory tone of postwar prosperity. Most of them led their respective industries, and most subscribed to the turn-of-the-century view that progress and the ethic of conservation were entirely compatible. Space was either sacred or profane, either reserved because of its special values or open to development. Few Americans challenged the dominant ethos of the postwar period—growth and development—and fewer still could do anything about it.

The powerful constituency that had supported the idea of conservation at the turn of the century had long given up the great influence it once wielded. Attrition, complacency, and the seductive smell of success had muted the emphasis on efficiency that once drove the movement, and the message of 1940s conservation sounded a little off to members of the class that used to form its backbone. Conservationists largely withdrew from national politics during the war, and in its aftermath they fragmented into smaller special-interest groups. Few groups with even a pretense of national standing remained. Most prominent was the Sierra Club, the Western-based, nature-oriented group still dominated by genteel white upper-middle-class members. Other groups, such as the Izaak Walton League, the Wilderness Society, and the newer National Wildlife Federation, mirrored the Sierra Club's demography and interests. The groups addressed only a narrow spectrum of issues: as late as 1950 the Sierra Club was—in the words of Norman Livermore, who went on to become state secretary for resources in California during Ronald Reagan's governorship—a fraternity of "rock climber types."

Although the war had forced people to conserve, the reasons were global—the shortage of rubber caused by the Japanese takeover of the East Indies, or the scarcity of sugar or gasoline—not because of any sense of efficiency, science, or even fear of profligate waste. As a political force, conservation all but disappeared. None of its leading organizations retained close ties to power. Conservationists offered a limited perspective and embraced an individualist style, born of the privilege of the roots of the movement. The postwar era was different in every way, and the means used to further conservation goals became archaic as Americans whizzed toward their future.

Even with a working organizational structure, conservationists lacked national vision and a clear point of view on the pressing issues of their day. Most leaders and organizations followed turn-of-the-century strategies, shaped in a moment when progress and preservation seemed compatible. They focused on issues of specific places, looked at scenery instead of urban blight, and seemed determined to protect only the "sacred spaces"—the national parks, the high mountain wildernesses, the distant rivers—instead of the communities where people lived. When they were heard at all, leaders sounded officious and silly, from another time. Conservation seemed outdated. It needed new tools to succeed in the postwar cultural environment.

By the end of the war the Sierra Club had begun to develop a politically active strain. The craggy and sometimes irascible David Brower, who would drive the transformation of conservation into environmentalism in the United States, led the way. After a difficult childhood in the San Francisco Bay Area, Brower dropped out of college in 1931, worked for the Curry Company, the concessionaire at Yosemite National Park, and in 1933 received his first Sierra Club committee appointment. By 1947 he was a veteran: he served on the organization's board and edited its official publication, the *Bulletin*. Brower's *Bulletin* differed from its predecessors. It screamed of activism, of real world issues and problems. Through it the revitalization of the Sierra Club tradition and its reformulation took shape.

No issue interested Brower more than the politics of land management, and his insistent coaxing led the Sierra Club to a new stance. Protecting wilderness became its initial political issue. Wilderness presented Brower with a range of advantages as he pushed the group toward political activism. The combination of progress as a value and social outings in the mountains clearly could not sustain a conservation organization as rapid development permanently altered the face of the American landscape. Brower gave protection of the mountains, loosely thought of as wilderness preservation, an urgency, and this new idea found a place alongside the High Trip in the Sierra Nevadas as characteristics of the Sierra Club.

Other organizations supported the idea of wilderness, but none had the reach of the Sierra Club. The Wilderness Society, founded in the 1930s by Aldo Leopold, the foremost early advocate of wilderness in the federal government and the creator of the land ethic in his book *A Sand County Almanac*, had made the preservation of wilderness its mission; but in its early years it functioned as a small club, a think tank that did little to influence policy. Like the Sierra Club, the Wilderness Society was genteel and, in the increasingly rough-and-tumble world of development politics, ineffectual. Nor did its leadership see political power as a goal. As the 1940s ended, most of the leaders of the Sierra Club, the Wilderness Society, or any other major conservation organization remained unconvinced that confrontational politics were right for their organization. Even with such active leadership as David Brower provided, the Sierra Club failed to respond with vigor to his calls to defend the wild. Instead the club remained rooted in the class-based, archaic form of clubbiness that emphasized outdoor experience, not protection. The Sierra Club directed its ener-

gies toward providing psychic achievement and moral sustenance for its members. Despite its Progressive era roots, it did
not focus on conservation or preservation in any of the classic
senses of either word.

The Wilderness Society shared similar problems. Both organizations had internal traditions that made them timid in
the public arena. As a forum for discussion, the Wilderness
Society gained early acclaim, but translating its ideas into policy was a more complicated undertaking. Since it did not as-
pire to a broad constituency, the society lacked an effective
public voice and had little influence on policymakers. Only
with the ascent of Howard Zahniser to the organization's
leadership after World War II did the Wilderness Society
begin to develop the traits that made it a viable political force.

Countermanding the growing interest in political conservation was the Bureau of Reclamation, which over the past two
decades had gained more influence than any other resource
management agency in the federal government and had become a serious competitor of its old rival, the Army Corps of
Engineers. Beginning with the 726-foot-high Boulder Dam in
the late 1920s, the agency had charted an aggressive course
that gave it preeminence as the federal government expanded
and promoted development in the American West. The Bureau of Reclamation was best positioned to inherit the mantle
of symbolic achievement, the role of the builder of great
American technological monuments that testified to mid-
century concepts of the national will, as the power to transform landscapes passed from private industry to the federal
government. Under President Franklin D. Roosevelt and his
secretary of the interior Harold L. Ickes, the bureau grew
from about two thousand employees to more than twenty
thousand. Inextricably linked to Morrison-Knudsen, Bechtel,
Brown and Root, and the other important Western construction and development companies, the bureau amassed great

power and, in the words of historian Donald Worster, "took pleasure in pushing rivers around." The Bureau of Reclamation built dams, often as political pork, and in an ongoing boom used federal dollars to support the regional economy. Under commissioners Mike Straus and his successor, the charismatic Floyd Dominy, a "forty-year binge" of federal dam-building, as critic Marc Reisner called it, lasted into the 1970s.

Massive reclamation projects that generated hydroelectric power in addition to providing water for reclaimed agricultural land became the forte of the Bureau of Reclamation. Beginning with Boulder Dam, renamed the Hoover Dam, and eventually including dams on nearly every major river in the West, the bureau pursued a program that linked government funding and local economies in a tight embrace. Providing water for irrigation and drinking, and generating hydroelectric power sufficient to light every city in the nation and make industry run, dam projects exemplified the development-oriented national philosophy that stemmed from World War II. This idea and the point of view it espoused led directly to the confrontation over the Echo Park Dam and the transformation of the old conservation ethic into a new and more politically potent form.

Proposed as part of the Colorado River Storage Project (CRSP), the Echo Park Dam inside of Dinosaur National Monument became the galvanizing issue that paved the way for the modern environmental movement. CRSP was a string of nine dams planned by the Bureau of Reclamation as a way to control stream flow, allocate water for agriculture, ranching, and increasing urban use, and create hydroelectric power to support growth in Utah, Colorado, New Mexico, Arizona, and Wyoming. Western congressmen and senators were used to lining up for largesse provided by the Bureau of Reclamation, a situation that its chief, Floyd Dominy, understood and successfully used to his agency's advantage. The bureau placed a premium on its role as providers of civilization's tools. And success made the bureau arrogant, even unbearable. Its leaders believed that institutions such as national parks ought to give way to the provision of services that promoted the common good. In the 1950s their perspective was widely shared; secretaries of the interior Julius Krug (1946–1949) and Douglas McKay (1953–1956) both agreed that national parks could be developed if the change achieved goals for the nation that were more important than the preservation of parkland. This approach differed from the view of pre–World War II secretaries of the interior, most of whom were closely tied to conservation. Under Krug's and McKay's policies, a project with national import could take precedence over even a congressionally established national park area. In the hands of development-oriented officials, the concept of national importance became quite subjective.

The instrumental philosophy of officials such as McKay meant that national parks now depended on the political process in a fashion that many park advocates found offensive. As a result of skilled leadership, the park system had become an asset to all the nation, widely regarded as apolitical in its formation, goals, and structure. The crown jewels of the system—those areas designated national parks—had been selected according to a loose set of standards that accentuated their unique attributes. Selections transcended local politics and politicos, and influential leaders of all stripes hesitated at the prospect of making park creation a political function. As national importance was conceived in the immediate postwar era, it was a relative measure—easy to claim and difficult to dispute. Dams in particular were easily presented as nationally important in the context of the cold war with the Soviet Union, at its height in the 1950s. Dams powered American atomic and nuclear testing programs; they symbolized American industrial confidence and might, and the energy they produced was reassuring in the face of the Soviet threat. They served as a linchpin of growth, creating a stronger national infrastructure that stood as a bulwark against external and internal threats alike. Under postwar standards of national significance, the burden of proof fell not on proponents of proposals such as dam projects but on those who defended the status quo. In the battle for Echo Park, that meant the National Park Service and the awakening postwar conservation movement.

Dinosaur National Monument was not among the jewels of the park system when it was selected for inclusion in the CRSP. Originally proclaimed as an eighty-acre paleontological site, the monument remained moribund until the late 1930s when a national park proposal instead yielded a national monument of more than 200,000 acres. Its remote location in far northwest Colorado and northeast Utah kept visitors away, and the monument languished. Despite its seeming lack of importance as an individual park, the principle at stake—the sanctity of designated areas—brought the Park Service in line with the conservation community.

By the time the Echo Park controversy began in 1950, the first post–World War II struggles over the sanctity of national park areas had already passed. In 1949 the National Parks Association (NPA), the Sierra Club, and the Wilderness Society fought the Glacier View Dam that the Army Corps of Engineers planned for Glacier National Park in Montana. The organizations won, defeating the Corps and concocting a strategy that, while successful, later came back to haunt its advocates. Olaus Murie, then president of the Wilderness Society, decided to support dam projects proposed outside of park boundaries. This he hoped would protect park areas from intrusion. The strategy seemed winning: it promised no opposition to projects outside of parks, so that dams and other developments could proceed without public outcry. It also created a de facto distinction between sacred space—land marked as having intangible value for aesthetic, recreational, and other purposes—and profane space, lands with economic utility that were open to development of all kinds.

In the context of the early 1950s this seemed a fair trade-off. Conservationists lacked genuine clout and enjoyed even less political power. Advocates shared a widespread sense that as a social goal, preservation had been accomplished. Most conservationists agreed that the most important areas were already preserved and that protecting them against intrusion seemed a wise and achievable goal. A combination of limited vision and a fear of consequences created a circle-the-wagons mentality aimed at consolidating earlier gains.

Despite the emergence of this tacit strategy, the Park Service could not publicly support conservationists at Dinosaur National Monument. The Department of the Interior supported the dam, and the Park Service officials who voiced their objection paid a political price. After Director Newton P. Drury publicly stated the Park Service's opposition to the dam, Krug's successor as secretary of the Interior, Oscar Chapman (1949–1953), silenced him. Chapman supported both dams proposed for Dinosaur National Monument, and soon after he forced Drury to resign. The next permanent director, Conrad L. Wirth, a development-oriented landscape architect with twenty years in the Park Service, had a long history of developing amenities in parks and usually found opportunities for development in any situation. The Park Service thus offered only a muted response to the Echo Park Dam.

With the Park Service hamstrung, the conservation community took on the lonely task of defeating the dam. David Brower and Howard Zahniser of the Wilderness Society took the lead. Drury's forced departure was an implicit threat to every unit in the park system, opponents of the dam agreed, and they planned to take their case to the widest possible public. The entire Colorado River dam package still required legislative approval, and beginning late in 1950, 78 national and 236 state conservation organizations mustered their supporters for an all-out assault. The largest groups organized lobbying, engaged in direct-mail campaigns, and even made a color motion picture that was shown hundreds of times across the country. Wallace Stegner, the noted author and historian, edited a book-length collection of essays and photographs that argued for keeping Dinosaur National Monument wild. Newspapers and national news and feature magazines presented the dam controversy at every opportunity. The Echo Park Dam became front-page news.

The nature of this war of words revealed significant changes in American society. By the early 1950s a strong undercurrent of dissatisfaction had taken shape. Progress had been wonderful to Americans, but its costs had been high. Increasingly expecting life to meet certain qualitative standards, many Americans at first seemed perplexed by the idea that their economic needs might interfere with their psychic ones. Many wondered, quietly at first, if establishing new and firm limits and adhering more completely to existing ones was more than just a good idea.

Out of this idea of limits and the prospect of loss came the gradual transformation of conservation into environmentalism. The battle against the Echo Park Dam introduced a newly revitalized conservation movement, more political than at any time since the turn of the century and developing its own set of issues, distinct from the efficiency ethic at the core of Progressive era conservation. For decades conservationists had become reluctant to use the political tools at their disposal. With activists such as Brower and Zahniser, leaders who

lacked close ties to power and did not fear offending others of
their class, this reluctance disappeared. The new conservation
movement aggressively challenged the dam and its backers,
seeing in democratic politics and the sense of loss that its leaders felt had begun to spread over American society an opportunity to reshape the debate over resource management.

Supporters of the dam used an argument that reflected
long-standing intraregional politics. Residents of Utah and
Colorado believed that without the dam their water would
continue downstream unimpeded to California, which would
use what it needed and let the rest flow into the Pacific Ocean.
With California-based organizations such as the Sierra Club
taking the lead in fighting the dam, representatives of the
upper basin states framed the conflict as an insidious way to
maintain the colonial relationship between powerful California and the weaker inland river states. Arousing public opinion against California was always easy in the Southwest and
the mountain West, and it helped create a fictitious division
between people of the interior West and Californians. Some
who might not have thought the dam a good idea supported it
when they saw it framed as a battle with California.

Conservationists responded by stressing their national constituency as well as the broader basis for their objections. The
dam in the park was not a regional issue, they insisted. It
tested the sanctity of national parks as well as the authority of
congressional decisions. People across the country opposed the
Echo Park Dam, conservation groups were prepared to
demonstrate, because of the aesthetic value of the canyon and
because of its designation as a national park area. Progress was
good, opponents of the dam allowed, but not in every canyon
and crevasse.

By taking the battle over the dam to the public, conservationists effectively circumvented both the Bureau of
Reclamation and congressional supporters of the project.

Preservationists worked quickly, for the Senate and House committees making the decisions were loaded with pro-dam Western Congressmen. The Bureau of Reclamation had strong support, particularly in the Senate among Joseph O'Mahoney of Wyoming, Clinton P. Anderson of New Mexico, Arthur Watkins of Utah, and Eugene Millikin of Colorado. The bureau's driving force, the vaunted, cigar-chewing Floyd Dominy, already on his way to becoming the most powerful federal bureaucrat in the West, had wide influence and support on Capitol Hill. Only an unparalleled public outcry could stop the dam.

With mail to Congress late in 1954 running at 80 to 1 against the dam, the Eighty-third Congress postponed its decision on the CRSP bill. Growth in the West had butted up against the growing discomfort of Americans with rapid and seemingly unstructured change that often appeared to benefit only limited segments of society. There were consequences to actions such as damming a river in a national park, a growing segment of the public believed, and those ramifications needed to be considered before the bill was acted upon. As Congress adjourned in 1954, Speaker of the House Joseph W. Martin, Jr., announced that the controversy over the dam had killed its chances for passage. Friends and foes alike awaited the new Congress.

In the Eighty-fourth Congress, with Lyndon B. Johnson as the new Senate majority leader, no issue more thoroughly dominated its early days than the resolution of the Echo Park controversy. Efforts to fashion a compromise failed, and support for the dam's opponents grew. Secretary of the Interior McKay, known by the sobriquet of "Giveaway McKay," had been closely tied to development and timber interests during his tenure as governor of Oregon, and there was every reason to expect Interior to support the dam. Surprisingly, the new director of the National Park Service, Conrad Wirth, voiced his objections to the project. Most expected him to be a friend of the dam. At the Senate hearing, Brower, by then executive director of the Sierra Club, eloquently voiced a range of objections. He exposed the fallacies in the bureau's scientific data, demonstrating that even the calculations of the evaporation rate of water from the pool behind the proposed dam at Dinosaur were inaccurate. Under a barrage of hostile questioning, Brower offered a powerful challenge to the economic rationale that underlay the dam proposal.

The project that had once seemed a certainty had now become deeply mired in politics. Although Senator Richard Neuberger of Oregon proposed that the Echo Park Dam be eliminated from the CRSP bill, the powerful Arthur Watkins of Utah battled him. In the end the Senate, where the lightly populated upper basin states were overrepresented, passed the CRSP bill with the Echo Park Dam intact. The House, more susceptible to pressure because all its members faced reelection every two years, passed a bill without provisions for the controversial dam. The battle continued as representatives from the Colorado Basin states met on November 1, 1955, in Denver to discuss ways to revive the Echo Park project. One of the main opposing organizations, the Council of Conservationists, placed a full-page open letter in the *Denver Post* which delivered a bold ultimatum: if the Echo Park Dam were put back into the CRSP bill, conservationists would oppose the entire ten-dam project with all the force they could muster by any legal means; if that one dam were eliminated, they would not oppose the rest of the project. Although some charged that the strategy was blackmail, the move trapped the proponents of the dam, forcing them to accept the terms or in essence battle against their own interests. From that point the resolution of CRSP without the Echo Park Dam proceeded with comparatively little difficulty. A viable compromise had been reached, and on April 11, 1956, the new bill became law.

The battle to stop the dam in Dinosaur National Monument touched a national nerve, raising questions about Americans' smug faith in progress. Defeat of the dam became a pivotal moment in challenging the course of American society. The decisions of a powerful federal agency and the support of local congressmen had been overcome—testimony to the increasing power of both public opinion and a Congress willing to assert the concept of national interest over home rule. Parks and wild land within individual states had been saved over the objections of representatives from those states. Local values were superseded by national ones as people who lived far away from Dinosaur National Monument played an instrumental role in blocking the dam. Many in the conservation movement at the time, and many who have written about the controversy since, have celebrated the demise of the Echo Park Dam proposal as a major triumph for the conservation movement.

This admiring view fails to account for the damage that could still be done to so-called sacred lands from outside their boundaries as well as to those lands that, for whatever reason, had not yet received protective sanction. While the Echo Park controversy may well have been the battleground on which modern environmentalism was born, the scope of the battle pinned the movement within narrow limits.

5

The Rise of Aesthetic Environmentalism

"FROM THE ANTS in our petunia beds to the crabgrass on our lawns, we will fight them off with chemicals till the grass and weeds are gone." To the tune of the *Marine Hymn*, so sang the generation of American children who came of age in the 1960s with television. They were responding—with the sarcasm of the young and powerless—to the sense of control that Americans had assumed over their land, but they reflected the clash between different varieties of American obsession. On one hand, across the nation, many Americans managed their lawns as if their lives depended on it; but while this cultivation evoked the agricultural past, it was largely an attack on nature. Chemical fertilizers, lawn supplements, plant nutrients, and endless rows of seed spreaders manicured the American lawn, made it orderly and demanded a kind of visual conformity that conferred status upon the family with the most orderly, clipped, and managed patch of grass in the neighborhood. Here was an opportunity to control nature—on a small scale—and simultaneously recall the mythic roots of Americanism. An American dad in control of his lawn was much more than a dad. He was a pioneer in the urban wilderness.

For precisely this reason, children responded with their own anthems that mocked and mimicked the goals of adults.

Forced to participate in the mowing and managing of the lawn as a post–World War II version of the household and farm chores once expected of the young, the privileged youth of the era resented the demands of their time and the expropriation of their labor. In the way that farm families once fought over who would haul the water for cooking, cleaning, and washing, postwar families argued over who would care for the yard, in what way, and especially about monetary compensation. While some loved yardwork, most hated it. Their disdain was not for the grass itself, but for the nature of the work and its goal of uniformity. This thinly veiled contempt was one more way for youth to distance themselves from the mainstream concerns of American society, one more way to show both the independence and the rethinking of values that the entire upheaval of the 1960s embodied.

The children's transformation of the *Marine Hymn* also illustrated the single most important condition that helped create quality-of-life environmentalism: the tension with progress that permeated American society after the splitting of the atom. Both awed and shocked by nuclear power, Americans lost their trust in science but continued to believe that technology promised a future free of risk. This promise proved to be false, dangerous, and frightening, and when Americans recognized that the very progress that was to free them also fouled their lives, they reacted with fierce resistance. Combined with other problems that seemed both incongruous and correctable in the most affluent society on earth, this tension helped spawn the cultural and political upheavals of the 1960s.

As a generation of young people, raised in the cushy affluence of post–World War II economic expansion, sought to perfect American society, they attacked its traditional ways of thinking, acting, and being. The nation became more self-centered; many Americans abandoned the last vestiges of deferred gratification and committed themselves to personal comfort and pleasure in a manner that pundits came to express as "freedom." In this process they transformed the nation: instead of continuing the sense of shared obligation that had underpinned American efforts during World War II—and not incidentally had been crucial in the formation of the conservation movement at the turn of the century—the nation took on an adolescent-like selfishness and petulance, a concern for the self at the expense of the larger whole. By the end of the 1960s most of the taboos that had been enshrined in American law and custom had disappeared. New symbols drove American culture, and many of the rules of American society had been cast aside or at least thoroughly revised. Americans wanted it all . . . right now, and a new ethos, the primacy of the individual, defined the nation.

The redefinition of American society was reflected in *environmentalism*, a political, cultural, and sometimes even revolutionary social movement. As with earlier American efforts at reform, such as the Great Awakening of the 1740s and the abolitionist movement that helped bring on the Civil War, Americans embraced the idea that they could perfect their world. Much of this energy focused on human problems—racism, poverty, inequality, sexism, and similar issues—but a great deal of it was directed toward saving the planet from the excesses of the human race. Although that energy took many forms, they all aimed to improve the quality of life. Human beings were entitled to clean air, clean water, open spaces, and a pristine and inspiring environment as well as to the life, liberty, and pursuit of happiness enshrined in the United States Constitution. Together these sentiments became environmentalism.

Environmentalism differed from the older conservation movement in myriad ways. Where conservation was obsessed with the efficient use of resources in a finite world, environmentalism grew from postwar affluence and envisioned an idealized utopia of untrammeled nature that lifted spirits and lightened the load of modern life. In this it resembled the thinking of John Muir, and took him from the fringe he long inhabited to a central position in the cosmology of environmentalism. Sixty years after his death, Muir's views became far more important than they had been during much of his life. While conservation had focused on society, on the greatest good for the greatest number in the long run, environmentalism often had ambiguous social connotations. It reflected the growing obsession with individualism that had come to dominate American society, but it also embraced a contradictory sense of community effort in support of collective goals.

Even the adherents of the two philosophies differed. Conservation attracted elites, who were often key players in the very controversies that stirred their movement. Environmentalism attracted idealists, many of whom were far from the sources of power and saw the world in the absolutist terms of the sixties. Environmentalists associated themselves with salvation in a near-religious fashion; there was an evil, they said, and only human faith—not the scientific knowledge of the conservationists—could save the earth and all its inhabitants from self-destruction. At times environmentalists sounded a clarion call, but their jeremiads could alienate as well as entice.

Environmentalism fused with the other reformist sentiments of the sixties, but it became one of the most enduring ideas of the era. It spoke to the American mainstream: despite its moments of revolutionary fervor, environmentalism was closely tied to a historic American optimism, a sense of destiny in the land, and a belief in the innocence of Americans. No better example existed than the evolution of the sentiment that humanity might be happier in simpler circumstances. Codified in movies such as *Easy Rider*, a cult film about two young motorcycle riders in search of themselves and their society, and acted out by young people who flocked to communes and other similar living arrangements across the country, this sentiment reflected the tension about progress now rampant in American society. Environmentalism provided the least threatening way to articulate the fear of growth and change, far less so than the radical Students for a Democratic Society (SDS) and their extremist splinter group, the Weathermen, who sought to overthrow the American government and resorted to violence to achieve their ends. Couched in rhetoric about the special nature of the American land, and tied closely to an aesthetic tradition that stemmed from the great landscape painters of the nineteenth century, political environmentalism sounded patriotic at a time when other challenges to the dominant culture seemed to argue for the unraveling of American institutions and the wholesale transformation of American society. While political radicals preferred to throw the baby out with the bathwater, young environmentalists often projected a genuineness that made adults find in them a sense of real purpose that they rarely granted student protesters.

The 1960s took on an almost anarchic tone. Some young Americans, especially the beneficiaries of progress and prosperity, seemed determined to cast them aside in pursuit of the murky if idealistic objective of spreading the wealth throughout American society. Some Americans turned their back on materialism and consumer culture; others challenged the rigid order of the social structure. Americans took economic growth for granted, and their prosperity encouraged them to regard it as less important. Many questioned whether the material gains of the moment were worth the long-term consequences of the destruction of nature.

American society in the 1960s was a remarkably optimistic place, fully sure of its position and with abiding faith in its problem-solving ability. President John F. Kennedy's "Camelot" offered a dreamy idealism—despite the many flaws underneath its shimmering exterior—and the nation and especially the young embraced it. The themes of Lyndon B. Johnson's "Great Society"—the end of poverty in America for all time, envisioned in the War on Poverty; the desire to eradicate diseases such as smallpox that had forever vexed humanity; the creation of programs such as Head Start to offer underprivileged children a better chance to succeed; even the campaign to reduce the number of billboards on American highways—revealed a supreme confidence and the widespread belief that human effort could create positive change. With so many benefits to industrial life, how could people fail to strive for solutions to its problems?

With the focus of that change so thoroughly on questions of the quality of life, 1960s environmentalism quickly took on the shape of middle-class culture. Its primary direction, articulated by many of the most dramatic thinkers and writers of the time, had nothing to do with subsistence but with protecting the options, prerogatives, and privileges of the middle class. The most popular environmental books, Secretary of the Interior Stewart Udall's prescient *The Quiet Crisis*, Rachel Carson's stunning *Silent Spring*, and Paul Ehrlich's *The Population Bomb*, all clearly articulated the enormous loss that had followed from human actions. The television commercial that featured "Iron Eyes" Cody, an elderly Native American with tears in his eyes at the littered mess that America had become, offered the same theme in the context of popular culture. The human race needed to assess its actions more carefully before continuing along the paths it had chosen.

Stewart Udall, Secretary of the Interior under presidents Kennedy and Johnson, provided an early and influential voice that questioned the triumphant American technology over the natural world. Assisted by the writer Wallace Stegner, Udall began to write after he became secretary. His book, *The Quiet Crisis*, published in 1963, challenged the notion that Americans, with all their technology and wealth, could do as they pleased in the natural world. From the arid state of Arizona, Udall reintroduced the idea of scarcity into American discourse, the sense that the world and its attributes were finite and that people could exhaust them. At the turn of the century Frederick Jackson Turner had alerted Americans to this idea as it applied to the frontier, and Progressive era conservationists clearly understood it, but since the end of World War II Americans had used technology to avoid limitations. Udall drew scarcity back into the national dialogue.

On the surface, Udall's solution was the same as that of the Progressives. He too looked to science to find objective, attainable solutions to the problems society faced; persuading a society to see those solutions in holistic terms was more difficult. "The swift ascendancy of technology has made the scientist the surest symbol of conversation in the 60's," Udall wrote. "His instruments are the atom-smasher, the computer, and the rocket—tools that have opened the door to an ultimate storehouse of energy and may yet reveal the secrets of the stars." Udall also recognized how the technological successes of science created dissonance between people and place. "The promised land of thousands of new products, machines and services has misled us," he continued. "Intoxicated with the power to manipulate nature, some misguided men have produced a rationale [that] might be called a Myth of Scientific Supremacy, for it rests on the rationalization that science can fix everything tomorrow."

Udall touched a chord with Americans who were increasingly uncomfortable with the consequences of progress. The atomic bomb had shown them that war was now an exercise in technological achievement, involving every aspect of a society and making everyone complicit. J. Robert Oppenheimer, legitimately the father of the bomb for his role in its wartime creation at Los Alamos, New Mexico, was forced from his position of scientific leadership in the mid-1950s as a result of his resistance to the idea of a hydrogen bomb, politicizing science in a way that belied its claims to objectivity. The search for more powerful technologies won out over the impulse to restrain, but one casualty was the unflinching belief in science as a medium of the truth. Progress acquired a tarnish that it never entirely shed.

As Udall illustrated, this ambivalence was articulated in many ways in American society. It was not enough to believe in science alone. Americans had to understand the social dimensions of their onward rush, the sense of loss and disorientation that so pervaded modern society. The disjunction appeared in the emphasis on back-to-nature movements that permeated the 1960s, in the optimism and sense of perfectibility that inspired the Great Society programs, and even in the words of the remarkable Martin Luther King, Jr., the civil rights leader who warned the nation, "Modern man suffers from a poverty of the spirit. . . . We have learned to swim the seas like the fish, to fly like birds in the air, but haven't yet learned to walk the earth like brothers and sisters."

Despite controversy, nuclear power became the basis for weapons production in the cold war era, and later an important source for civilian power needs. An arms race followed the explosion in August 1949 of the first Soviet atomic device. By then the United States already had a well-developed atomic testing program in the Bikini Islands of the South Pacific. In 1946, Operation Crossroads, the code name for the first tests, had begun to assess the effects of radiation by loading abandoned ships and depopulated islands with fruit flies, goats, pigs, and rats. Test Baker in the Crossroads sequence, an underwater test, brought especially surprising results. Scientists assumed that high levels of radiation fallout would persist for only a few days following a bomb blast. After Baker, the entire area, including the abandoned ships known as "target vessels," the fish in the water, and even the air, showed high levels of radiation well beyond expectations. To the dismay of scientists, soldiers sent onto the bombed vessels with buckets and brushes to scrub away the radiation did not reduce the levels at all. The question of atomic fallout loomed increasingly large.

The realization that atomic radiation was far more dangerous than previously thought shook the scientific community and created genuine fear. Task force physician David Bradley concluded in his 1948 book *No Place to Hide* that for fallout from nuclear explosions there were "no satisfactory countermeasures and methods of decontamination." In 1949 the two hundred Marshall Islanders who had been evacuated from Bikini Atoll were told that they would never be allowed to return to their homes. Radiation was a powerful by-product of atomic technology, a legacy that proved uncontrollable.

Above-ground testing, both in the Bikini Islands and in the Nevada desert, became the rule during the massive arms buildup of the 1950s and early 1960s. Testing escalated in both technological capability and size as bombs became more sophisticated, more numerous, and immeasurably more powerful. Much of the testing was done as a way of flexing national muscle, each side demonstrating that it could destroy the other with a dazzling array of nuclear weapons. At the Nevada test site, roughly 90 miles from the budding resort and gaming community of Las Vegas, no less than 126 above-ground tests were carried out between 1951 and 1961, before the 1963 international ban on above-ground testing. After the ban, tests continued below ground, the occasional rumble of the earth signaling the occasion to residents of a wide region around the facility. In 1961, near Carlsbad in southeastern New Mexico, a 3.1-kiloton bomb was detonated below ground in one of the many caverns that dotted the area. In the Bikinis, above-ground testing continued until the ban took effect. Testing left a radioactive legacy that would persist for at least 10,000 years, later prompting the label "national sacrifice zones" for the testing sites.

By the early 1960s the United States and the Soviet Union each possessed the ability to destroy the world many times over. A generation of schoolchildren had been raised to fear nuclear attack, and a sense of threat hung over the nation, accentuated by the 1962 Cuban missile crisis. Meanwhile the American landscape seemed increasingly toxic, even as a generation worked to clean it up. A paradox faced American society: the very technologies that made life better generated hazardous waste and toxic by-products—from chemical spills to radioactive fallout. That progress could simultaneously be so beneficial and so threatening befuddled the nation.

The quality-of-life movement also contained a powerful element of aestheticism. This was the conviction that the American middle class was entitled to live a life that, while free of risk, also enriched the soul. The promise of technology had been freedom, purchased in the transformation of raw material into goods. Americans had long overlooked the downside. In short this meant that middle-class Americans expected the marvelous bounty of their society, but assumed that there were no consequences—or that others would face them. This made the prospect of untoward consequences even more threatening when people such as Rachel Carson pointed them out.

Personally shy and reserved, Carson helped awaken American society to the dangers of agricultural and household chemicals. She had an exceptional ability to explain science in clear and graceful writing, rising through the Department of the Interior to become editor-in-chief of its publications while she pursued a writing career on her own time. Her first book,

Under the Sea-Wind, appeared in 1941 to public acclaim. The
New Yorker magazine serialized her second book, *The Sea
Around Us*. It remained on the *New York Times* best-seller list
for months and became a primary selection of the Book-of-
the-Month Club. The book's success allowed her to leave government and become a full-time writer.

Trained as a biologist, Carson had watched the application
of synthetic pesticides to crops, rangelands, and other habitat
with horror all her adult life. American agriculture had long
used natural fertilizer such as dung and guano, and the spray-
ing of arsenic on selected crops was well established by the
early twentieth century. "Spray, farmers, spray with care/
Spray the apple, peach, and pear/Spray for scab and spray for
blight/Spray O spray and do it right," ran the E. G. Packard
poem that summarized the farmers' practice. In the mid-
1920s, responding to serious health hazards, the Food and
Drug Administration (FDA) tried to set standards for the
amount of arsenic left on fruit crops, but it was thwarted by
the industry and by bad publicity.

As in many other areas of American life, World War II
initiated a revolution in the use of synthetic chemicals.
Inorganic compounds such as DDT (dichloro-diphenyl-
trichloroethane), a potent insecticide first synthesized in 1943,
found wide usage. New phosphorous insecticides, such as
malathion and parathion, also became popular. By 1947 the
United States was producing more than 125 million pounds of
such chemicals each year. When researchers took samples of
soil and water across the country, they nearly always found
traces of these chemicals. Chemical poisoning had been a possibility since the nineteenth century, but inorganic chemicals
increased both the number of potential problems and the frequency of residues.

By the mid-1950s, when Carson received a letter from her
friend Olga Owens Huckins that crystallized her nagging

concerns, the consequences of the widespread use of synthetic chemicals had begun to affect American life. Huckins made a poignant complaint: from her kitchen she could no longer hear songbirds in the morning. This complaint focused Carson's attention and led her to write *Silent Spring*, which succinctly captured a fear tied to the quality of life: one day, dawn would break over a prosperous nation and not a single songbird would be heard.

Silent Spring created a national sensation and made the reclusive Carson a celebrity. The book indicted the chemical industry, agribusiness, and the federal government for the indiscriminate use of chemicals and inspired a loud and usually partisan response from every corner of the respectable world of industry and science. Defenders of the status quo circled the wagons. *Time* magazine accused Carson of an "emotional and inaccurate outburst," and Ezra Taft Benson, formerly secretary of agriculture and later president of the Church of Jesus Christ of Latter-day Saints, attacked her status as a single woman, suggesting that the book resulted from her lack of personal fulfillment. Department of Agriculture officials, agribusiness, and the chemical industry saw the book as a vast public relations problem. Members of the professional science community, the researchers who supported the development of synthetic chemical remedies, believed Carson's work disparaged their credibility. What Carson condemned as a "Neanderthal age of biology" was the dominant mode of insect control and the course of income for many industrial scientists, not to mention the funding of their research, the stature of their profession, and, for many, their own self-esteem.

Carson rubbed an exposed nerve in American society, setting off responses from the White House on down. *Silent Spring* was published in September 1962 and became an immediate best-seller. More than 600,000 copies circulated in its first year. Stewart Udall publicly supported Carson, and his efforts led President Kennedy to promise an investigation of Carson's charges even before the book was available in stores. Despite a letter-writing campaign designed to discourage the project, in the spring of 1963 CBS aired a prime-time special entitled "The Silent Spring of Rachel Carson." Carson had made the toxicity of progress a national issue.

Carson's axiom that "We know not what harm we face" spoke to an important legacy of technological innovation in American society. The technology that freed Americans was wonderful but it was dangerous. Nor could humans depend on themselves to limit their use of dangerous technology. After *Silent Spring* and a generation of atomic and nuclear testing, Americans tacitly understood that little was beyond the reach of the human race. If people devised a new technology, good, bad, or indifferent, sooner or later they would use it. The question was not really if, but when.

Of course, not all technology was to be feared. The problem was far more complex. Technological innovation added immeasurable, sometimes wonderful advantages that contributed to widespread changes in social mores. The most prominent of such technologies was the birth-control pill, which debuted in 1960. It promised women a kind of sexual and reproductive freedom they had never enjoyed. It also offered a potential solution to another problem that surfaced in the sixties. In 1968 the biologist Paul Ehrlich published *The Population Bomb*. It built on the argument first offered in 1798 by the English philosopher and cleric Thomas Malthus, that if population grew exponentially while food production expanded only arithmetically, the planet would soon be overpopulated. Ehrlich believed that technological advances allowed more people to survive childhood and thus significantly lengthened life, placing humanity on the road to self-destruction. In his view, the sheer weight of natural increase doomed the planet. In the most famous section of his book,

Ehrlich explained the source of his understanding. It came "emotionally one stinking hot night in Delhi," India. In the more than 100-degree heat, amidst dust, smoke, and the rancid smells of humans and animals, Ehrlich wrote, "The streets seemed alive with people. People eating, people washing, people sleeping. People visiting, arguing, and screaming. People thrusting their hands through [our] taxi window, begging. People defecating and urinating. People clinging to buses. People herding animals. People, people, people, people." From that night on, he believed he knew how overpopulation felt. Ehrlich wanted to transmit that feeling to Americans, to show what he thought the future of the nation would become if Americans did not restrain themselves.

The third environmental sensation of the decade, *The Population Bomb* sold more than three million copies and began an immense debate about the number of people the planet could hold. Attacked as a prophet of gloom and doom, Ehrlich forced a range of people across cultural and religious boundaries to take long-term consequences into consideration as they fashioned social, cultural, and even religious policy and doctrine. He raised the question of equal resource distribution as well as the problems inherent in engineered solutions to infant mortality, disease, improved agricultural yields, and other conditions that had long affected the species.

Ehrlich's position challenged the Roman Catholic Church as well as everyone who believed in programs such as the Green Revolution, which transferred American seeds, technology, and pesticides to the people of the Third World in an effort to help them produce better crops. Catholic doctrine in the 1960s opposed all forms of "artificial" contraception, but such methods of birth control were already common in the Western world. Americans remained notoriously laggard in considering the implications of their own population growth, preferring to regard overpopulation as a function of poverty rather than of resource consumption. Americans could afford babies, many seemed to be saying; it was the rest of the world that could not.

The ideas of another of the major environmental thinkers of the 1960s, the biologist Garrett Hardin, also confronted the issue of scarcity, this time from the position of social behavior and its consequences. In 1968, in a presidential address to the Pacific Division of the American Association for the Advancement of Science entitled "The Tragedy of the Commons," Hardin voiced a revolutionary thought: some classes of problems could not be solved by technology. This idea ran counter to the faith in science that still reigned in American society but also spoke to the ambivalence Americans felt toward technology. As the source of their problems, it also remained the potential solution. Hardin believed that Americans needed to reexamine their individual freedoms to see which ones were defensible in light of burgeoning social needs.

Hardin made his point by demonstrating the problems encountered by societies with shared common resources. He regarded human beings as maximizers of opportunity, using commonly held resources first and saving their own until the shared ones were depleted. There was only one Yosemite Valley, to which everyone had unlimited access; this access led to an erosion of the very values that people sought from the park—to congestion in Awanhee Meadows, for example, and to a string of climbers across the face of El Capitan. In 1969 a riot in Stoneman Meadows on the Fourth of July crystallized Hardin's critique. The Yosemite Valley seemed cramped and cluttered. Common areas like this, Hardin argued, were justifiable only as long as population remained static. As soon as numbers rose, for whatever reason, rules that protected common areas fell by the wayside. In the ever more densely populated world, Hardin insisted, people needed more rather than fewer rules to govern their activities. Greater freedom for all would ultimately result from this sacrifice of individual liberty.

The second half of the twentieth century became the age of the individual in American society, and in it Hardin fulfilled an eccentric role. For better and worse, the right to do what one pleased—wherever, whenever, however, and with whomever—came to be the social definition of freedom. No more basic American right existed. The famed expression of 1960s angst, "Do your own thing," elevated the individual over any social objective, perceived or real. At a time when Americans were learning to distrust their leaders, Hardin advocated commonly agreed upon solutions in the form of rules and laws—in other words, government—to solve the social problems produced by overpopulation. As did almost everything during the 1960s, the problems and the best solutions to them seemed irreconcilable.

Despite its obviously politically liberal position, Hardin's formation became classed as conservative. It argued for limits on individuals at a time when student radicals and the musicians and popular culture heroes who carried their message wanted to, in the words of one Jefferson Airplane song, "Tear down the walls" and free the young from the restrictive structures of society. The back-to-nature movement, comprised of people who embraced the ideals of the counterculture but fled urban streets for the seemingly bucolic and idyllic rural life, where they would raise their own animals and grow their own food, reflected the enormous influence of individualism. Singing songs that preached freedom from social constraints, its members were unlikely to request government approval before exercising as basic a human right as having children. If anything, they were likely to defy restrictions. The Jefferson Starship, a spin-off of Jefferson Airplane, expressed this sentiment in "A Child Is Coming," a song about the ensuing birth of a baby to a couple who are hooked on freedom. "What are we going to do when Uncle Samuel comes around, asking for the young one's name?" the chorus begins. "Looking for the print of his hand for his file in their numbers game. I don't want his chances for freedom ever to be that slim," the song continues. "Let's not tell them about him." The definition of freedom as the liberation of the individual from any socially devised restraint ran directly counter to the ideas of thinkers such as Hardin and Ehrlich.

In this context the idea of communal rural living held great promise. It seemed to free the individual from the rules of society, the clock-punching, mortgage-paying routine that promised nothing more than a dulling of the senses and the death of the spirit. Young people from the suburbs populated these communes. All came with an idealized vision of the nature of rural life, but most of them knew little if anything about agriculture or animal husbandry, the basics of their adopted existence. Occasionally such places survived, usually by the skill and ingenuity of a dominant leader and the discovery of a specific product to market rather than by the development of a subsistence economy. But most failed, some dismally. In their wake they left disillusioned and sometimes devastated individuals who, lacking the skills necessary for the life they had chosen, found their ideals dashed by the harsh reality and fundamental poverty of their rural experience. Even the communes that survived for a significant time, such as the Taos Commune in New Mexico, experienced constant turnover. The back-to-nature mythology of the 1960s ran hard against the day-to-day grind of machinery-based and borrowed-capital rural life.

Such experimentation was equally noble and foolish, an attempt to address what many saw as the ills of success, a correction to the unfettered growth and expansion of technology, the suburbs, and the dominance of automobiles across the nation.

It reflected a changing national value system, a reassessment of the virtues and vices of the nation as the two hundredth anniversary of the signing of the Declaration of Independence in 1976 approached. Despite the transformation of the nation into a world economic power, the development of a massive physical plant and infrastructure to support industrial society, and many other advances, Americans had real doubts about the success of their endeavor. Having more of everything, they expected more—of their leaders, of themselves, of their land, of their culture.

Out of the nation's uncertainty, environmentalism emerged as a compromise position, a center from which the striving toward a new consensus in American society began. The long-standing bipartisan consensus in Congress about conservation contributed to this movement of an idea to the center, as did the state of American skies and water. Even in the most privileged places, the places where people enjoyed the enormous wealth that industrialization had created, untoward consequences were often visible and always at least hinted at. It was impossible to turn on the TV, read a newspaper, or live one's life without being exposed to pollution of the air, water, and land, to the rumble of jet airplanes, to the sound of pneumatic jackhammers and the smell of leaded exhaust. For almost everyone, the goals of the environmentalism were difficult to resist. In principle, environmentalism reflected the desires of the nation.

First Lady Claudia "Lady Bird" Johnson's "Keep America Beautiful" campaign defined the way environmental goals became national goals almost overnight. Her interest reflected both her personal love of the outdoors and her and the president's affinity for their rural roots, as well as a growing concern for the littered American landscape. In the 1960s her position did not permit her to function as a policymaker, but it did cede to her issues of social and moral concern. In this role Lady Bird Johnson became a primary advocate of a number of aspects of the new environmentalism, such as the cleanup of U.S. highways, programs to beautify urban areas, and the development of a beautification strategy for inner-city neighborhoods and schools.

Lady Bird Johnson became the symbol of the beautification movement. She enjoyed considerable influence over her husband, and he was a powerful and persuasive president until Vietnam destroyed his credibility. Her activities broadened the constituency for the goals of environmentalism. Poised and gracious, she made a fine symbol in a time of turmoil, and many people found beautification significant simply because the First Lady believed in it. The program had as many symbolic as actual ramifications. It made the environment a key social issue and identified it closely with mainstream politics.

Another factor in the increased importance of the environment as an issue was the rise in consciousness about pollution. A historic problem with roots in the transformation of humanity from nomadic to sedentary peoples, and aggravated by industrialism and urbanization, air and water pollution was everywhere in the late sixties. Leaded fuels, chemicals, wastes, and other sources seemed to threaten everyone's quality of life. The air made people wheeze and their eyes tear; the aroma of industry was everywhere. New synthetic detergents, developed after World War II, created immense amounts of non-water-soluble foam. As early as 1947, sewage plant operators reported unprecedented foaming. The sources of local drinking water, rivers and lakes throughout the land, soon became suds-laden and polluted. Government efforts to combat the problem began in the 1950s, but effective regulation took a full decade. Industry lobbyists held up legislation until 1965, when Congress limited the manufacture of synthetic detergents, curtailed importation, and monitored the soap industry.

Foaming soaps were phased out, and by the mid-1970s non-foaming linear alkyl sulfonate (LAS) detergents dominated the market.

Foaming soaps also challenged American cultural values. By the 1960s, Americans had become routinely accustomed to newer and better versions of every household product. Synthetic detergents suggested that the consumption-oriented American way of life might not be tenable. More might not always be better. But detergents were a familiar commodity, one that Americans considered a necessity. When technology created a better detergent, the larger issue of convenience versus quality of life was easy to ignore. Americans could have both. Pollution was controllable—at least until a larger disaster forced the nation to grapple with harder truths.

On January 28, 1969, the blowout of an oil-well platform off the coast of Santa Barbara, California, made pollution real for the American public. The Pacific coast at Santa Barbara was one of the most stunning areas in the United States. The affluent resort and university town, originally a Spanish pueblo and in the 1920s a resort for the superrich, was charming, innovative, and seemingly removed from the trouble that wracked the nation. The blowout changed its ecology in an instant. It spilled 235,000 gallons of crude oil, blackening thirty miles of white sand beach. The Santa Barbara spill threatened the myth that Americans could have it all, and resonated through the nation.

Santa Barbara was well insulated from the worst features of modern industrial life, a fact that made it an ideal symbol for the quality-of-life revolution sweeping the land. Pollution typically had been confined to industrial plants or to neighborhoods of blue-collar ethnic workers and minorities. Many Americans who depended on industries that fouled their nests found it difficult to protest. Prosperity and risk had gone hand in hand with industrialization. The pallor that hung over industrial towns was the price of the newfound affluence of the industrial middle class. Santa Barbara residents, on the other hand, luxuriated in their Eden, enjoying the wealth no small number had wrung from the haze that enveloped the rest of the nation. When pollution invaded a sanctuary of privilege, public and private consequences were certain.

Although pollution problems were apparent enough when they reached someone's backyard, genuine solutions were not as easy. Most critics fell back upon the anti-establishment rhetoric of the sixties, pointing to the flaws in the "system" instead of seeking answers to problems resulting from the awkward embrace of risk and prosperity. Americans would not give up their opulence to assure a pristine environment. Instead they wanted a clean environment and an ever-increasing standard of living. It was not within the realm of public policy to conjure a way around this most basic of American predicaments.

The Santa Barbara oil spill accelerated the push to regard questions of pollution as serious public policy issues and helped bring the environmental movement closer to the American mainstream. After Santa Barbara, Americans understood pollution, either as a result of a disaster or because of constant endemic conditions, as a threat to the quality of life. Despite Garrett Hardin's observation that technology could not solve all problems, Americans resorted to it. And when it failed to deliver, they began the hard and slow process of considering changes in the way they thought and lived. Environmentalism found center stage in American culture, increasingly symbolizing the hopes and dreams of Americans who believed the perfectibility of their society was at hand.

By the end of the 1960s, environmentalism had taken its place among the important symbols of American society. It quickly cropped up in mass media of all kinds. Iron Eyes Cody confirmed that, despite the efforts of Lady Bird Johnson, the American landscape was not as beautiful as Americans perceived it had once been. Its shores were covered with broken glass, its highways littered with food wrappers and bottles. The symbolism of the man dressed as a mythic Indian chief conveyed many things: the passing of obligation from the so-called first ecologists to modern people, who had clearly abdicated their responsibility; the reverence with which Americans in general were beginning to regard the Native American past; and the simply disastrous condition of the American landscape. The appropriation of this symbol played an important role in bringing environmental issues closer to the mainstream.

Other iconographic characterizations helped assist the transformation. The green ecology symbol typified the popular response. Public symbolism played an important role in the 1960s, and many people literally wore their beliefs on their sleeves. The peace sign was only the most familiar of such icons. The ecology sign, made popular at the end of the decade, reflected the rise of individual interest in environmentalism and the public affirmation of its importance.

Smokey Bear, whose utterance "Only you can prevent forest fires" became one of the most oft-repeated phrases of the era, claimed a place in the American heart. In 1950, after a devastating blaze in New Mexico's Lincoln National Forest, a firefighter named Homer Pickens had found a badly burned black bear cub that he and his friends initially called "Hotfoot." When the cub healed he was rechristened Smokey Bear, after a fictional bear the Forest Service had invented as a promotional figure during World War II to remind campers to care for the forests, in no small part because timber was needed for the war effort. Smokey's plight made headlines, and after his paws healed he found a home in the National

Zoo in Washington, D.C. There he became so popular that he was assigned his own ZIP code. Americans, especially children, flocked to see him, and with the dissemination of books, signs, and other material emblazoned with his face, Smokey Bear became a beloved American icon, a symbol of responsibility and stewardship.

As a symbol, Smokey reflected the goals of the U.S. Forest Service, charged with managing the vast national forest tracts. Smokey's axioms, "Crush out your butts," "Break matches in two and hold till cold," and "Always drown your campfire," taught environmental responsibility to children through the remarkably pleasant device of a friendly animal with human characteristics. Loved and lionized, Smokey the Bear became another of the iconographic figures whose message supported the ideas of environmentalism.

Popular music also began to reflect environmental themes. No song more poignantly expressed concern than Marvin Gaye's stunning 1973 hit "Mercy Mercy Me (The Ecology)." "Where did all the blue skies go?" Gaye sang. "Poison is the wind that blows from the north and south and east. . . . Oil wasted on the ocean and in our seas, fish full of mercury. . . . Radiation in the air and in the skies, animals and birds who live nearby are dying. . . . What about this overcrowded land? How much more abuse from the man can she stand?" Gaye poignantly encapsulated the range of fears of the environmental movement.

By the early 1970s environmentalism had become a forceful social movement in the United States. Even Barbie now sported synthetic instead of real fur as a nod to the environmental movement. The middle class had had its say. Quality of life was significant in American society. The question still loomed: how would that attitude be translated into policy and law?

6

The Limits of Quality of Life

THE QUALITY-OF-LIFE MOVEMENT was a middle-class phenomenon, and as the latest in a long series of similar movements in the United States, it seemed virtually guaranteed of success. There were really only two ways to create fundamental and lasting change in the nation. One was to make an argument of such powerful moral suasion—like Martin Luther King's in the 1960s—that the nation could not help but respond. The other was to find a theme that struck a chord with the middle class. Here was the simple key to the success of quality-of-life initiatives: they had both the sanction of the middle class and the force of its vast but often slow-to-coalesce influence in American society. The combination made the 1970s the "environmental decade."

At the same time the emphasis on quality of life left out large segments of the American population. Although the nation had been living with a comprehensive nuclear weapons complex since the 1940s, and although steel, chemical, paint, and other plants continued to weave together prosperity and dangerous toxic side effects, the focus of environmentalism remained narrow, away from where people sometimes did the dirty work of life. One reason was certainly that much of the middle class had moved away from industrial work into white-collar professions. For relatively low-skilled workers, earning better wages often meant accepting high levels of risk in industrial situations. As prosperity became commonplace, an unspoken bargain developed between industry and its workers. A job in the industrial workplace came with a silent lifetime guarantee. Workers expected cradle-to-grave benefits, and in return they tacitly accepted the risks of the industrial workplace, exposure to chemicals and solvents along with the risk of injury from machines. That acceptance extended beyond the factory to the noxious effects of industry in the neighborhoods—air pollution that defoliated gardens, dumping grounds filled with waste of various kinds, and similar hazards. As long as the bargain between workers and industry held, complaints from victims were few and far between. Everyone knew where their prosperity came from, and adults who had grown up in the depression of the 1930s knew how fleeting it could be.

This dangerous bargain split the potential constituency for environmentalism at precisely the moment of its greatest success. On the one hand, in an affluent society the possibility of preserving land and resources was greater than at any time in American history. Simply put, people believed that no one would be hurt by creating wilderness or protecting endangered animals. The goals of a middle-class movement, usually achieved through legislation, had the effect of maintaining the old sacred-profane distinctions of the conservation era. David Brower's strategies were typical: define a place as special and then draw a line around it, protecting it for all time. This solved the significant short-term problem of preventing despoliation, but as the battle for Glen Canyon showed, it left open larger questions. In this formulation the onus remained on environmentalists to demonstrate why land should not be developed. It also left environmentalists concerned almost exclusively with places where people did not live.

On the other hand were the problems of an industrial society and its impact on the daily life of ordinary people. The nascent anti-pollution movement was decidedly urban, its voices often muted by the close relationship between affected people and polluting industries. The goal of this movement was nearly opposite that of the wilderness advocates: instead of drawing a box around special places, the anti-pollution movement concerned itself with the entire nation. People such as Marvin Gaye linked the injustice of racism and poverty with the problems of the earth. These problems were everywhere, Gaye observed in his music, effectively reversing the wilderness advocates' point of view. The anti-pollution movement insisted that *all* places should be free of hazards, placing the onus on industry to prove why people, American citizens especially, should endure such conditions.

Yet this cry was muted throughout the 1970s, a direct result of the unspoken agreement between workers and industry. Risk was part of the bargain, assumed by workers who believed they had been properly cautioned and who understood the risks involved in the work that paid for their homes and educated their children. If subconsciously they understood they might be making a potentially great sacrifice, such people were accustomed to sacrifice. Accepting the bargain guaranteed their livelihood. It was a fair trade, one that built risk into the fabric of American life as long as the industrial workplace could sustain blue-collar families with rising aspirations.

In the United States the twentieth century became the regulatory century, and translation of environmentalism from a concern of the middle class into law provided one of the foremost examples. Throughout the century, federal involvement in regulation consistently grew. By the end of World War II the regulatory role of government was secure. Although some quarters in American society occasionally displayed a fierce resistance to the idea, Americans generally expected that federal support for everything from roads and buildings to health-care programs came with stipulations.

After World War II, and especially after 1960, environmental regulation was among the most pervasive controls in everyday American life. Traditional environmental issues such as wilderness preservation were the first to be sanctioned in the legal code, quickly followed by the regulation of pollution of the kind that had fouled the beaches of Santa Barbara, California, limiting the way in which commodities such as oil were transported. A complex array of environmental regulations and agencies to enforce them grew, redefining the relationship between humans and the physical world in the most affluent society on the planet.

Among these the Wilderness Act stood out. Its passage in 1964 initiated a revolution in the nature of environmental legislation. Unlike any previous law with general application, the Wilderness Act permitted the reservation of land that had little economic value for a sole purpose—its own preservation. During the ensuing fifteen years, similar pieces of legislation stood a greater chance of becoming law than ever before or since. The Wild Horse and Burro Act of 1971 and the Endangered Species Act of 1973 served as the foremost examples. They ensured the reservation of land for species without regard to economic cost.

The decision permanently to set aside land from commercial economic development was the product of a period of remarkable prosperity for the nation. The optimism that fueled the Great Society played out in the environmental dimension as well. People believed they could set aside land because their opportunities were so great that the material advantages of any single tract would scarcely be missed. A nascent spirituality, tied to the utopianism of the 1960s, also shaped the passage of bills like the Wilderness Act. Americans recognized that

wilderness—for many just the *idea* of wilderness—helped
make them whole, helped obviate the sense of loss that
stemmed from urbanization and suburbanization. In this respect the people of the 1970s were not far from their anti-
modern, Progressive era antecedents. Together with other
factors such as the back-to-nature movement, these attitudes
combined to make the Wilderness Act and subsequent legislation central to American aspirations.

The battle for wilderness protection began with the Echo
Park Dam fight and became a decade-long struggle. Howard
Zahniser, executive director of the Wilderness Society, played
a leading role. A quiet man who earned his spurs at Echo
Park, Zahniser understood Washington, D.C. In the discontent with unbridled development that came to the fore during
discussions of the dam, Zahniser pushed for a wilderness system with standing in federal law. At Zahniser's behest, Senator Hubert Humphrey of Minnesota and Representative John
Saylor of Pennsylvania introduced the first wilderness bills in
1956, during the second session of the Eighty-fourth Congress.

With development the dominant characteristic of the era,
wilderness legislation faced complicated but surmountable
barriers. Increased affluence and the time to travel combined
to bring millions of Americans to national parks after the war,
and within a few years national park and national forest
campgrounds overflowed with trash, litter, tire tracks, and
cigarette butts. In the 1950s national parks were forced to
serve increasing levels of visitors with the resource capabilities
of the late 1940s and a physical plant designed to meet the demand of the 1930s. Bernard DeVoto, a noted historian and
journalist, argued that if the government would not care for
the national parks, they should be closed. This radical pronouncement achieved DeVoto's objective: an uproar that attracted the attention of an increasingly conservation-oriented
public.

From DeVoto's work and the powerful alliance of Western congressional leaders came Mission 66, a ten-year capital development program to refurbish the national parks in time for 1966, the fiftieth anniversary of the founding of the National Park Service. For the Park Service, the program was a windfall. The House and Senate competed to fund visitor centers, permanent homes for staff, roads, campgrounds, and other developments. For congressional representatives, park amenities were another way to subsidize states with federal dollars in an era when legislators measured their success by the projects they delivered back home. Nearly every park in the system benefited from Mission 66; its most visible legacy remains the dozens of post-office-like visitor centers that dot the park system. Congressional representatives found their support of such projects to be the basis for returning to office time and again and accruing power during long stays on Capitol Hill.

While Congress and the public enjoyed the benefits of rescuing and developing the national parks, Zahniser and his friends sought a law that ran counter to such goals. Wilderness demanded a different understanding than did recreational development. In a coat with so many pockets that some called him a walking file cabinet, Zahniser strode the halls of Congress, buttonholing one congressman after another, persuading a senator here, beseeching a staff member there for a moment of his representative's time. The tireless Zahniser kept the bill in play, session after session, well into the early sixties. One obstacle he faced was the recalcitrance of the federal agencies that would receive responsibility for designated wilderness areas. None of the agencies, the Park Service, the Forest Service, and the Bureau of Land Management, were thrilled with the prospect of a wilderness bill that limited their discretion and seemed to create more complicated, more expensive management. Changing circumstances wore down their resistance. In the optimism of the Kennedy and Johnson years, anything seemed possible, and environmentalists reflected the utopian spirit of the time. Under David Brower's leadership, the Sierra Club came forward to lead the drive for wilderness legislation.

When President Johnson signed the Wilderness Act into law in a ceremony in the White House Rose Garden on September 3, 1964, it was truly a victory for the environmental movement. It mandated the creation of a wilderness system selected from federal lands that would be reserved from all forms of development. Although Howard Zahniser died of a massive heart attack shortly before the act was passed, the law was his legacy. He had been the indefatigable bureaucrat, even as wilderness philosophers such as Aldo Leopold and Robert Marshall received intellectual credit. There was a delicious irony in Zahniser's posthumous triumph: not the activist, not the philosopher, not Muir, not Leopold, but a bureaucrat who built support through perspiration instead of inspiration had made the difference. The Wilderness Act taught advocates an important but often overlooked lesson: working inside the system achieved greater results than railing from the outside.

The passage of the Wilderness Act signaled the arrival of environmentalism. Wilderness was a true quality-of-life issue. Even most of its advocates never went anywhere near it, but its psychic importance as an indicator of the health of the world and the virtue of American society was great. Out of the various pieces of conservation interest, Zahniser and Brower successfully interpreted the hopes, fears, and aspirations of American society and forged a new movement that tugged at the emotions of the most influential portion of the American public, the broad and prosperous middle class of the late 1960s. While it maintained a de facto fidelity to the old sacred-profane distinction, the new environmentalism found a constituency that reflected its values with energy and clarity.

Through the 1960s the environmental crisis, as it was soon known, rose on the scale of American concerns. The problems seemed vast and almost incomprehensible, and the remedies available ineffective at best. As the nation changed political direction and accepted new cultural values, government served two functions: it was on one hand "Big Brother," the oppressor, but it was also the means through which to rectify problems. Those who favored government intervention won out in public policy arenas, for in the aftermath of events such as the Santa Barbara oil spill and a later noxious air mass that trapped toxic smokestack emissions in Birmingham, Alabama, government reprised a role it had played during the Progressive era. It was the one institution in American society with enough power to take on major corporations and natural resource conglomerates.

In a figurative instant, quality-of-life environmentalism jumped onto the list of federal priorities. The transition occurred abruptly, reflecting a shift in the public psyche. In 1968 the Brookings Institution did not list ecology, environment, or conservation among the issues that demanded the new Nixon administration's immediate attention. But within one year the environment, pollution, and quality of life became prominent themes in the political process and issues of national scope and importance. Senators Gaylord Nelson of Wisconsin and Edmund Muskie of Maine led the way in Congress, and a spate of legislation forced the reluctant Nixon administration into assuming a stance as defenders of the environment. When President Nixon gritted his teeth and signed the landmark National Environmental Policy Act of 1969 (NEPA) after it sailed through Congress, it marked a significant turning point. Even a Republican administration felt compelled to respond to the widely felt need for environmental protection.

The passage of NEPA reflected the importance of the environment to American voters. Environment had now become a social issue, a health concern, and an aesthetic responsibility rolled into one buzzword. Americans believed that the protection of their environment was a socially advantageous and highly desirable goal. The passage of NEPA created a set of obligations that reflected the message from the public to its leaders: environmental quality was a standard of measurement in American life.

Among the many provisions of NEPA was the requirement that an environmental impact statement (EIS) accompany every federal or federally supported development. The EIS became the pivotal step in the process of legal compliance established by the new law. The requirement introduced new and higher levels of public oversight never before experienced by federal administrators. Simultaneously it allowed citizens to challenge projects on the basis of environmental impact. EIS documents were open to the public, and each EIS draft was followed by a round of public hearings. Under ideal circumstances, the EIS process offered a comprehensive view of environmental impacts of federal projects to the president, the cabinet, executive-level advisers, and the public. NEPA demanded new levels of accountability from federal projects.

NEPA also established the Council on Environmental Quality (CEQ), the highest legal advisory body to the president on environmental affairs. Created with an exclusively advisory capacity, the CEQ had its mission thrust upon it. The president determined its role and could make as little or as much use of it as he chose. Initially Nixon avoided the CEQ, but members of the council did not sit by and wait for directives. Instead they shaped not only the president's legislative agenda on the environment in 1971 and 1972 but many other environmental decisions as well. Under some leaders and in some administrations, the CEQ could be assertive. In other cases, such as during Ronald Reagan's presidency, it simply waited for instructions.

Environmentalist sentiment gathered remarkable momentum and changed the pattern of government action in only a few years. Nixon's first Message on the Environment, another NEPA-inspired directive, came in February 1970. A few months later Congress terminated the Supersonic Transport (SST) project because of its environmental consequences, negating almost $1 billion of earlier support. At about the same time Nixon brought the $50 million Cross-Florida Barge Canal to a halt—it was the first project ever stopped because of its impact on the environment. The decision shocked the powerful Army Corps of Engineers, which had expected to construct the canal and was rarely thwarted. But economic growth was no longer the sole objective of national policy; a cleaner environment, a clear representation of the idea of quality of life, had gained tremendous support and comparable importance.

In December 1970 the establishment of the Environmental Protection Agency (EPA) set a new standard for environmental protection in the United States. For the first time a "line agency," a federal agency with its own independent budget, assumed responsibility for environmental issues. Another NEPA by-product, the EPA was the centerpiece of the emerging federal environmental regulatory system. It supplanted agencies such as the Federal Water Quality Administration in the Department of the Interior and the National Air Pollution Control Administration located in the Department of Health, Education, and Welfare. It also administered the many solid-waste management programs scattered throughout the government; set standards and guidelines for radiation control, a task formerly the province of the Federal Radiation Council; and handled pesticide and toxic substance registration and administration. With a $2.5 billion budget by 1972 and more than seven thousand employees, the EPA became a powerful arsenal closely tied to the bipartisan coalition that comprised American environmental politics.

With the establishment of the EPA, the federal government codified an environmental ethic into both policy and the legal code. The EPA's creation sent a new message to the public, suggesting that formal oversight would redefine the administration and use of the American environment. With its broad and comprehensive power, the agency inaugurated a new era in which the federal government assumed responsibility for environmental conditions in ways that had never before been expected or required by law.

From the perspective of environmentalists, the environmental impact statement process contained a number of significant flaws. The EIS itself was only a document, not the solution to every environmental problem on the planet. It could be manipulated for all sorts of purposes. As one former Department of the Interior official noted with a twinkle in his eye, "You could write an environmental impact statement that said the consequence of an action would be to destroy the world and that there were better alternatives than that action, and the action could still go forward." In other words, the process had its limits. It lacked the power to halt destructive actions, only requiring that they be evaluated and explained. Environmental impact statements became the most important document in the initiation of any federal undertaking, but sometimes superficial research and faulty reasoning took the place of clearheaded analysis and substantive, comprehensive documentation. The EIS often became a malleable document, tuned to the needs of constituencies that sought development and less useful in resolving environmental issues than the framers of NEPA might have envisioned.

No situation illustrated these limits as clearly as the building of the Trans-Alaska pipeline. In 1966 Walter J. "Wally" Hickel, a multimillionaire real estate developer, contractor, and hotelier who was a huge proponent of development, won the governorship of Alaska by a mere eighty votes. Hickel promised to open up the state to development, with oil in the forefront of his plans. The reasons were obvious: in 1965 oil and gas production had boosted mineral extraction above federal military expenditures as the leading source of Alaska's income. With confirmation that almost ten billion barrels lay under Alaska's arctic regions, plans to open up the north began in earnest. In 1967 the governor commissioned a four-hundred-mile highway from Livengood, about sixty miles north of Fairbanks and the end of the line for public roads in Alaska, across the Brooks Range to Sagwon, about ninety miles short of Prudhoe Bay. It was a bold and impulsive move, an economic fiasco that carried little freight and an ecological disaster that destroyed the tundra and awakened the first opposition to oil development in Alaska.

Shortly after Hickel was nominated as secretary of the interior by incoming President Nixon, the Trans-Alaska Pipeline System (TAPS) announced plans to build a pipeline to carry crude oil from the vast fields around Prudhoe Bay. The decision to construct the pipeline happened just as environmental issues were reaching a critical mass in the offices of government, and the pipeline became embroiled in both changing American attitudes toward the environment and quality-of-life issues, and the legislative revolution that transformed the way Americans dealt with the physical world. Although application for the permit to construct the pipeline preceded NEPA, during 1970 the pipeline fell under the jurisdiction of the statute. It also became part of the ongoing question of Alaskan native claims to land. Even as it got under way, the greatest development project in Alaskan history found itself on the defensive.

The battle over the pipeline pitted development in the United States' last wilderness against growing national sentiment that favored preserving nature. On one level it was a question of the state's economic growth against the nation's desire for a pristine wilderness, a dilemma not unlike the one between the so-called first and third worlds after the end of the cold war. On another level it was the older American consciousness, admittedly rapacious, pitted against the ideals of the regulatory century. Could people still do as they pleased, unrestrained by law and custom, with the nation's natural resources? Many Alaskans, led by the charismatic Hickel, believed they could.

Attacks on the pipeline took three forms: administrative and legal challenges to the project were many, and Alaskan native claims in an era when Americans expressed remorse for the fate of native peoples were a powerful obstacle. Logistical and technological difficulties associated with building eight hundred miles of pipeline through the Arctic delayed construction. In June 1970, amidst lawsuits by natives and environmental organizations, and court injunctions, TAPS halted the project. The biggest endeavor in Alaskan history ground to a halt in the face of the environmental revolution.

The Environmental Impact Statement for the project became one of the major obstacles to construction. The pipeline project began as a consortium of ARCO, Humble Oil, and British Petroleum; five other companies joined in. As it became unwieldy, some pulled out. The remainder incorporated the Alyeska Pipeline Service Company as a nonprofit entity to serve as the lead organization to the project. Remarkably, with NEPA looming, no one considered the EIS an important issue. Early in 1971 proponents realized what a mistake they had made. When the pipeline EIS was made public in Washington, D.C., the 196-page document with a mere 60 pages of appendices set off a storm of protest. Astute individuals in the

Department of the Interior advised their superiors not to sign off on the flawed EIS. Numerous officials believed the document did not conform to the strictures of NEPA; others believed it constituted a fraud perpetuated on the American public. Testimony from the initial public hearings required by law ran to more than 12,000 typed pages. Before more than two years of discussion and revision were complete, an archivist calculated that stacked in a pile, the project's paperwork submissions would reach fifteen miles in the air. When the final environmental impact statement was released on March 20, 1972, it was a 3,500-page, 9-volume report that cost almost $13 million to prepare.

The final EIS was an unusual document, the first of its kind, and everyone read it from his own point of view. Proponents of the pipeline felt that it did not support the project strongly enough—though it affirmed the Interior Department's general approval of the project that had been included in the draft proposal. While the EIS described a range of potential issues—wilderness, seismic activity, and the numerous areas in which adequate information for assessing the project did not exist—opponents were dismayed by the lame challenge that the document offered to what they regarded as one of the most environmentally destructive projects in human history. Opponents filed a thirteen-hundred-page rebuttal in conjunction with their legal efforts to stop the pipeline, and even though Secretary of the Interior Rogers Morton announced a forty-five-day grace period to allow for comment, the tension remained fierce. The battle over the pipeline reflected a growing polarization in American society between advocates of the traditional American ethos of more, more, more and those who envisioned a more restrained society. How people lined up on the pipeline in many ways reflected how they perceived the future of the United States.

The arguments recalled the heated discussions between

conservationists and advocates of unbridled development at
the end of the nineteenth century. When former Secretary of
the Interior Stewart Udall, on a June 1973 speaking tour,
warned Alaskans against too much development without regard to its consequences, the Arizonan sounded to many
Alaskans as if he were a nineteenth-century Easterner casti-
gating the West for its development aspirations; the delicious
irony of a Westerner criticizing Alaskans was not lost on the
Northern public. After their difficult battle for statehood,
which came to fruition only in 1959, Alaskans regarded the
pipeline as the economic tool that could give meaning to their
status. This prompted vituperative response. In 1975 Terris
Moore, who had been president of the University of Alaska
from 1949 to 1953, blasted the Sierra Club and other environmental groups as the latest in a succession of colonial forces to
dominate the state. Moore took the analogy further, suggesting that statehood did for Alaska what the *Brown v. Board of
Education* decision had done for African Americans, and that
with their new freedom Alaskans should be permitted to
make their own decisions. Although the comparison was a remarkable stretch, Moore's argument suggested the depth of
Alaskan passion for the pipeline.

Even after its eventual approval by Congress in 1973, the
pipeline remained controversial. Environmentalists challenged it in court and in congressional hearings. But the Organization of Petroleum Exporting Countries (OPEC) oil
embargo constituted a national emergency that shut off Middle East oil and inexorably altered the politics of the pipeline.
As the embargo took effect, the price of gasoline soared, and
Americans waited in long lines at the pump, the pipeline
legislation sailed through Congress. Alaskan oil became a
quality-of-life issue imperative, but in a different fashion than
environmentalists had imagined.

The pipeline was constructed and in 1977 began carrying

oil across Alaska to the port of Valdez, eight hundred miles from where it originated. Even the most ardent pipeline proponents conceded that environmentalists and the EIS process had forced industry to provide a safer pipeline. Some believed that the four-year delay was worth the cost in dollars, trade deficits, and other economic measures; others believed the time had been wasted. Either way, a new era began. A combination of politics, perspective, the courts, and attentive groups and individuals made compliance with NEPA a reality, but in the end economic concerns won out. The legacy of the pipeline controversy became not environmental regulation but the fierce allegiance of Americans to their favorite personal transportation device—the automobile.

On April 22, 1970, a public celebration of a new kind occurred across the country. The first Earth Day showed how completely Americans embraced the idea of quality-of-life environmentalism. Combining the free-wheeling spirit and tactics of the 1960s and a reach across class, generation, race, and other lines, Earth Day began as a loosely connected series of environmental teach-ins—planned but informal sessions where people expressed their views—at colleges, high schools, and community centers across the country. From these disparate origins, Earth Day metamorphosed into a typical late-twentieth-century public display of belief in the United States.

The drive for Earth Day came not from the periphery of American society but from the very center of power. Senator Gaylord Nelson of Wisconsin, an outspoken advocate of environmental quality, created the context in which Earth Day occurred. He started a "National Teach-in on the Crisis of the Environment" at a September 1969 symposium in Seattle, and from there the idea gathered momentum. Nelson hoped to draw the environmental constituency together and limit its ties with New Left politics. He believed that the environmental crisis was the greatest dilemma the human species had ever faced, the one issue that crossed every social, cultural, political, economic, and geographic boundary. His teach-in began to alert everyone in the country to questions of quality of life.

As 1969 ended the teach-in had generated a great deal of attention and was poised to become the kind of vehicle Nelson had sought. The chief organizer of Earth Day, Harvard University law student Denis Hayes, made it a centrist event. He balked at confrontational politics, seeking to unite rather than polarize. "We didn't want to alienate the middle class," Hayes remarked later. "We didn't want to lose the 'Silent Majority' just because of style issues." The organizers fashioned Earth Day as a celebration of American society, a search for consensus as well as alternatives. This assured Earth Day a wide reach but undermined it with more activist constituencies. These groups regarded militance and activism as synonymous, and found the placid, cheerful nature of Earth Day a little bland.

Earth Day became a rousing success but only a mildly threatening challenge to the system. Environmental Action, which sprang from the teach-in, proudly described Earth Day as the largest, cleanest, most peaceful demonstration in American history. Mixing soft 1960s ideology, the rhetoric of moral suasion, and the tactics of the civil rights movement, Hayes created an approach that simultaneously included and excluded radicalism. In the environmental movement, he insisted, everyone had a stake, no matter what their politics.

Earth Day developed into an educational forum that usually included a convocation, singing, dancing, food, and rhetoric from environmental advocates. Politics also played a role; petitions that called for a halt to polluting industrial activities sometimes circulated among the Earth Day crowd, and political candidates with environmental values found willing audiences. The educational effort was also directed at a younger audience in the elementary school grades. In an instance repeated in almost infinite ways across the country, a sixth-grade class marched outside on a raw April day in Illinois to plant a tree on the school playground. Students stood around, thrilled to be out of class even for a few moments in the blustery wind, half-aware they were participating in an event of historic proportions.

What some called tepid confrontation, others regarded as the politics of inclusiveness, and this latter posture gave environmentalism its widest hearing in American society. Earth Day seemed a way to do more than complain; one could instead participate in renewal. This had the added effect not only of making people feel a part of something good and important, but also of reminding them that they could make a difference in their world. This feeling of personal power that so many derived from participation in environmentalism spread its message widely. The symbols of environmentalism caught on, and all kinds of Americans made its values their own. Businesspeople and activists together talked of the same goals; legislatures followed. The passage of bottle bills that offered a slight economic incentive for the return of glass containers led the way in representing this new point of view. For an instant, environmentalism became the center of a new nation, a place where all Americans agreed. Here was an issue that a wide range of Americans, from the leaders of industry to the political left, all saw the same way.

Throughout the early 1970s wilderness maintained its symbolic power in American society, enjoying a hold on the national imagination and a place in the minds of middle-class Americans. New technologies, many derived from the space program, allowed millions who could never before contemplate a "genuine" outdoor experience feel that such adventure was within their reach. American recreation was transformed:

with backpacks, freeze-dried food, and lighter, more comfortable gear and outdoor wear, middle Americans experienced the outdoors on their own terms. Wilderness and the outdoors in general became fashionable, a mark of belonging, of being part of the new and culturally revitalized American nation.

For many Americans, this growing interest in the outdoors included a new involvement in environmental organizations. In the 1970s existing environmental groups grew in size and many new ones sprouted, energized by the many laws now protecting the outdoors. As Americans suspiciously eyed their government after the Johnson administration's Vietnam debacle and the fall of Richard Nixon in the Watergate scandal, environmentalism steered clear of national politics. The outdoors was theirs, Americans seemed to say, and they guarded their privileges closely. New laws meant new opportunities for the public to view and comment on the management of resources, and Americans of all kinds let their views be known.

The new circumstances threatened the autonomy and prerogative to which federal agencies were accustomed. From the powerful Bureau of Reclamation to the more timid Bureau of Land Management, federal agencies found their decision-making challenged. In New Mexico a National Park Service planning team was greeted with loud public dismay after a recommendation of "No Wilderness" at Bandelier National Monument. The Bureau of Reclamation found its dam projects, once the epitome of pork-barrel politics, challenged by an aggressive public. The so-called "water buffaloes," powerful congressmen such as Wayne Aspinall of Colorado, for years chairman of the House Interior and Insular Affairs Committee and a great proponent of development, in the early 1970s found themselves run out of office. On the Navajo reservation, the Peabody Coal Company's EIS for a one-way slurry pipeline to carry coal to Page, Arizona, led to an increase from the pre-EIS price of $5 per acre foot for water to a cost of $600 per acre foot when it was renewed in 1987. The Forest Service faced repeated attacks on its wilderness policy. Agency officials tried to have it both ways, maximizing the timber cut from national forests as the public fought for roadless land in designated wilderness areas. The Roadless Area Review and Evaluation (RARE) process, designed to respond to the public, mired the agency in even deeper controversy and a range of legal actions.

Certainly the remarkable prosperity of the postwar era played an important role in creating this scenario, as did the reshaping of the American self that accompanied the 1960s cultural revolution. Many Americans began to see themselves less as denizens of work and more as creatures of leisure, entitled to expect more from their world in all kinds of ways. That sense of privilege, of new categories of rights, stretched from the workplace to the vacation home, from worker to hiker, from outdoor advocate to factory neighbor. It led, ever so gradually, to a growing resentment of the toxicity of prosperity that Americans had long embraced and endured.

The catalyst for much of the quality-of-life revolution was fear of the consequences of technologically induced abundance. Americans recognized that there was a price for the opulence of their life, but unless they were directly confronted with the consequences, they tended to look past threats of health and safety and see only benefits. Rachel Carson cracked the thin veneer of national self-deception with *Silent Spring*; the events, both environmental and political, that followed, and the changing culture that made it seem wise to mistrust authority, made many Americans worry about accidents in a range of industries that served them.

No industry generated more fears than nuclear power. Presented to Americans as a clean fuel that would generate electricity too cheap to be metered without fouling the air as coal-fired plants did, nuclear power gradually became anathema in American society. As much energy went into stopping it as went into opposing the Vietnam War, powerful testimony to the way it became regarded as a sinister threat to the nation. In essence, Americans, long accustomed to risk, decided they could not bear this one. This was a powerful transformation inspired by the quality-of-life revolution.

After World War II, civilian uses of atomic and nuclear power developed slowly. The United States possessed abundant resources for conventional power generation; dams like Hoover and Grand Coulee offered seemingly endless sources of electricity at minimal cost, and the sheer quantity of American coal seemed to preclude other forms of power generation. But the coal-fired plants created visible particulate pollution, and the sooty skies of the 1950s needed no help from fresh smokestacks. Atomic and nuclear power came into the civilian power scene as replacements for archaic coal plants, among the nation's greatest air polluters.

Even before the concern about polluted air, the federal government had experimented with nuclear power for civilian purposes. In the 1950s President Eisenhower promoted "Atoms for Peace," a project that used atomic power for construction as well as for electricity. Among its programs was Operation Plowshares, an attempt to use an atomic bomb to reshape the usability of natural features. The chairman of the Atomic Energy Commission, Glenn Seaborg, remarked that "nuclear explosives give us, for the first time, the capability to remedy nature's oversights." The ideas for such uses were plentiful. In 1946 Captain Eddie Rickenbacker, World War I flying ace and later the general manager of Eastern Airlines, proposed breaking up the ice of Antarctica with an atomic bomb; others proposed using atomic or nuclear weapons to deepen the Panama Canal. Underground explosions in the continental United States were supposed to create enormous amounts of natural gas; while tests, such as Project Gasbuggy in New Mexico in 1967 and Project Rulison underneath Colorado in 1969, did create natural gas, much of it was too radioactive ever to be harnessed. The promise of nuclear power blinded advocates to its drawbacks.

Nuclear testing took place in a conflicted cultural climate. Since sometime in the late 1940s, and certainly after David Bradley published *No Place to Hide* in 1948, scientists and the better-informed public were well aware of the dangers of radiation from atomic and nuclear blasts. Untoward consequences seemed to creep closer to home. In 1954 the twenty-three-person crew of the Japanese fishing vessel *Lucky Dragon* was irradiated near the Marshall Islands by fallout from a blast over Bikini Atoll, more than a hundred miles away. On September 1, 1957, Eisenhower signed the Price-Anderson amendment to the Atomic Energy Act of 1954, limiting the liability of the nuclear utilities industry as a way to make investment more attractive. This in itself suggested the potential for disaster, a potential made real eleven days later when a fire at the Rocky Flats Nuclear Arsenal in Colorado released thousands of times the allowable limit of plutonium into the atmosphere. When British epidemiologist Alice Stewart's demonstration of the carcinogenic effect of radiation on children was published in the *British Medical Journal* in 1958, the worries increased. The report of the United Nations Scientific Committee on the Effects of Radiation (UNSCEAR) that even the smallest exposure to radiation could have severe genetic effects, was followed by the discovery of elevated levels of strontium-90 in milk in the United States and consequently in children's bones. When the Waltz Mills test reactor outside of Pittsburgh experienced a partial meltdown in 1960, and a test reactor in Idaho Falls, Idaho, went out of control early in 1961, killing three technicians, the fear of nuclear power became palpable. Touted as a panacea for energy problems, nuclear power terrified Americans.

As a result, civilian nuclear development proceeded alongside conventional forms of power generation. As late as the early 1960s, coal-fired power plants were still being constructed to augment hydroelectric power, especially in the West. The massive coal-fired plant at Page, Arizona, on the Navajo Reservation, a project brokered by Utah Power and Light, was typical of non-nuclear development. But even as such plants proliferated, so did nuclear power plants. In 1957, the year the Soviet Union launched the Sputnik satellite and propelled a generation of American students to study science and technology in federally funded programs, the first American nuclear power plant, at Shippingsport, Pennsylvania, near Pittsburgh, took shape. By 1962 three other plants—Dresden, outside of Chicago; Yankee Nuclear Power Plant near Rowe, Massachusetts; and Indian Point Station, twenty-six miles north of New York City—were on-line. The USS Savannah, the first nuclear-powered merchant ship, was built at about the same time. By the mid-sixties nuclear power sources accounted for a greater percentage of the power produced in the United States than any other source. In 1967 nuclear power provided 46 percent of the sixty million kilowatts of electric power orders placed by domestic industry.

Quality-of-life concerns contributed to the growth of nuclear power production. As air pollution became an increasing problem, nuclear power seemed a viable alternative to coal-fired generation, an obvious source of considerable pollution. Nuclear power plants promised cleaner air, cheaper electric power (an important concern as the cost of coal and petroleum products rose), and what appeared to be an infinite source of power as the nation searched for new sources of fossil fuel. Federal funding supported the nuclear industry, and during the 1960s and early 1970s half of all power-plant construction in the United States involved nuclear reactors. When Jimmy Carter was sworn in as president in January 1977, nearly sixty civilian nuclear power plants were operating in the United States.

The atom sprang onto the American scene so quickly that attempts to understand, regulate, and manage it fell short. American society had no mechanisms for assessing the consequences of atomic activities. Especially when the military was involved, the claim of national security, heard often and vociferously throughout the cold war, squelched most complaints. Even civilian uses evaded scrutiny. The Atomic Energy Commission, a precursor of the Nuclear Regulatory Commission and the Department of Energy, functioned in complete secrecy without public oversight. Even above-ground testing within the continental United States received only minimal scrutiny until the end of the 1950s, when those who lived downwind from the Nevada Test Site began to question the impact of the ongoing tests. Sadly, the claim of national security did not prevent American officials and scientists from making decisions that some critics saw as calling into question the entire idea of nuclear power—and weapons. Beginning in the 1950s, when opponent J. Robert Oppenheimer and proponent Edward Teller—both nuclear scientists—clashed over the hydrogen bomb, and continuing through an era characterized as "radiant science, dark politics" by radical chemist Martin D. Kamen, a politically active scientist and one of the discoverers of carbon 14, the uses of radioactive material and its effects became more and more mysterious. The public was told simply to take safety on the word of people such as Teller. This demand for secrecy in near wartime conditions may have been necessary, but it tragically cloaked questionable, irresponsible, and even unethical behavior.

For the people who worked with atomic and nuclear materials, a sometimes haphazard decision-making process posed a genuine risk to their health and safety. The military was the source of much of this risk, especially to people near testing grounds or any of the numerous facilities involved in producing materials related to nuclear enterprises. Even in instances when officials recognized potential damage, little effort went into facing the problems these programs spawned. The safety of those who came in daily contact with radioactive material was simply not a priority. Workers at the Hanford Reservation in Washington State, where nuclear weapons were assembled, might be exposed daily; those who lived in the path of the winds that blew across the Nevada desert after aboveground testing, and even in such seemingly innocuous places as the Oak Ridge National Laboratory outside Knoxville, Tennessee, also ran inordinate risk. Neighbors of the Rocky Mountain Arsenal in Colorado, where throughout the postwar era poor monitoring and inadequate storage led to a series of leaks of chemical and atomic material into the surrounding environment, also faced danger. Unexplained releases of radiation poisoned cattle and sheep from Nevada as far north and east as Minnesota. Unusually high rates of atypical cancers and clusters of rare diseases appeared in central Washington, southern Utah, and a range of other places throughout the rural West.

Mostly people bore these threats to their health in stride. At mid-century and after, no American wished to be seen as a whiner or complainer, especially during the cold war. Atomic workers, their families, and the communities that depended on their wages were supposed to bear their risks as part of the bargain that sustained industry. Nor did the nature of the diseases that stemmed from exposure to radiation make complaints easier to demonstrate. With the exception of the most severe cases of exposure, most radiation-induced illness incubated in humans for a long time, as much as twenty years. Americans, then and now, planned for the immediate but neglected the long term. As long as large numbers of people did not experience immediate negative effects, the combination of secrecy and lack of a need for an urgent response dulled those complaints that did surface. But the number of affected people grew annually, and their voices became louder, leading the way to a revolution in values.

Despite its many advances, quality-of-life environmentalism had clear and obvious limits. At its core it was class-based, narrow in the main thrust of its interest to people with access to the amenities of modern life. It also seemed somehow selfish, full of the spirit that became known as NIMBY—"Not in My Backyard." Despite the many obvious points of connection among people who opposed nuclear proliferation or toxic poisoning, these strands, so often parallel with wilderness and other outdoor recreational interests, rarely intersected. Perhaps it was the decision of the founders of Earth Day that contributed to this centrist position; perhaps it was the fundamental obsession with the self that so characterized the 1970s. Whatever the reasons, despite its many advances, environmentalism remained confined in American society to the well off. In a moment of such affluence that it was genuinely possible to transcend class boundaries, environmentalism did not quite make the stretch.

A beneficiary of the full stomach of postwar American prosperity, conventional environmentalism ran up against its limits. Its message—that people should sacrifice and ignore the biological drive to maximize in order to preserve the future—offered little to those experiencing prosperity for the first time or those still longing for plenty. Nor did its message appeal to those whose future depended on technology: farmers, increasingly dependent on synthetic chemicals for higher crop yield; or industrialized workers who recognized that their prosperity was associated with risk. In its zeal to improve life, environmentalism had inadvertently drawn a fault line— between haves and have-nots—that would contribute to an enormous backlash against it.

7

Backlash: Full Stomachs and Empty Pockets

THE CURTAIN came down in a hurry on the optimism and prosperity of postwar America. The OPEC oil crisis combined with Vietnam War–related inflation to drive the cost of living up faster than at any time since the immediate aftermath of World War II. Worse, wages failed to keep pace in the inflationary climate. The end of postwar economic expansion hit all at once, epitomized by the rising cost of gasoline. At the peak of the oil embargo in the winter of 1973, Americans suffered the indignity of having to wait in line to fill up their automobiles. This unthinkable inconvenience heralded a new moment. In a figurative instant, the pillars of postwar prosperity—cheap energy, rising wages, and low inflation—cracked. Americans faced a new economic future, one with greater limits. Government offered an ineffective response. In the mid-seventies President Gerald Ford wore his WIN—Whip Inflation Now—button, but it was about all his caretaker government could offer.

Beginning in 1974 the United States entered a twenty-three-year period that essentially brought reduced prosperity to most Americans. The key statistic was the annual drop—for each of those twenty-three years—in the real value of hourly wages. Simply put, people worked longer hours to stay where they were on the socio-economic ladder. One-income families declined; each year it took more hours to make do, and middle-class women entered the workforce in greater numbers than ever before in American history. From 1945 to 1974 a typical income had bought more goods than Americans had ever experienced. Prosperity extended up and down the socio-economic ladder. When the era ended, the full-stomach phenomenon also came to a screeching halt.

The consequences of this shift and the effects of the burgeoning global economy were enormous for American workers. The nation lost entire industries—electronics in particular—retaining only specialty niches, and few returned in any viable form until after 1990. Before the 1970s, American companies such as Motorola and RCA sold television sets and other electronic equipment while Japanese goods were generally regarded as cheaply made. Now the American auto industry found itself almost in failure from Japanese and German competition. Poorly led, General Motors and Ford struggled with design and efficient manufacture, and the Chrysler Corporation was forced to ask the federal government for a bailout. Only after 1990 did prosperity return to the auto industry consistently. The Watergate scandal, when confidence in the political system reached an all-time low and cynicism toward American institutions became commonplace; a mid-1970s recession combined with runaway inflation late in the decade, when interest rates reached 21 percent; and, finally, what President Jimmy Carter described as a "national malaise," which eventually damaged his bid for reelection, left the nation stunned, shaken, and profoundly discontented.

Full-stomach environmentalism, the premise that the nation was free to make decisions based on the precept that almost everyone had almost everything they wanted and needed, became an anachronism almost overnight. In a changing economic and cultural climate, the prerogatives of this environmentalism now faced serious challenge and even ridicule. They seemed to be relics from a different, more af- fluent, and certainly more optimistic time.

The 1960s had opened up American society in many ways. As long as prosperity held, objections to change were muted. But in the late 1970s, with Americans held hostage in Iran, in- terest rates rising, and manufacturing jobs disappearing, those who had once been beneficiaries of federal largesse now found themselves in difficult straits. And now they loudly and pub- licly resented the transformation of American society. Affir- mative action, women's rights, and environmental regulation were seen as symptoms of decline and threats to the social order. The "revenge of the white male" became the first major challenge to bipartisan environmentalism since the Echo Park Dam controversy.

The resistance to environmental regulations appeared throughout the American landscape, but it especially per- tained to wilderness and the outdoors, the arenas in which people such as Howard Zahniser had fought so hard. It first became apparent in 1973 in the battle against the Endangered Species Act. One of the by-products of Americans' attitudes to- ward nature had been the wanton destruction of wildlife that accompanied expansion of the nation. All kinds of species, in- cluding the passenger pigeon that once crowded American skies, had become extinct, and countless others, such as the American bison, teetered on the brink of oblivion. Even the ubiquitous prairie dog was reduced to a relict population.

Protective measures for certain species had joined the pa- rade of environmental legislation during the 1960s. The En- dangered Species Preservation Act of 1966 provided for the protection and propagation of native species of fish and wildlife, from the largest vertebrates to the minuscule Devil's Hole Pupfish, a fish less than two inches long that lived in one sinkhole in Ash Meadows, Nevada. A later bill, the Endangered Species Conservation Act of 1969, expanded protection from vertebrates to mollusks and crustaceans, and extended protection from only those species facing extinction to those merely threatened by human encroachment. The Endangered Species Act of 1973, the final stage of this process, focused on the protection of "critical habitat" but did not define the term in a legal or administrative context. The limits expressed by the language of the act foreshadowed a growing tension in a nation forced to choose between economic and environmental goals that seemed mutually exclusive.

When University of Tennessee zoology professor David Etnier discovered a small fish called the snail darter in the Little Tennessee River in an area slated to be flooded behind the nearly completed $116 million Tellico Dam project, the Endangered Species Act became a center of national controversy. The snail darter debate became the first test of the ethic of bipartisan environmentalism, a struggle that pitted the hopes of the nation against its growing fears. The discovery kicked off a two-year legal battle. Opponents, backed by an interagency committee, called the dam a pork-barrel project; proponents blamed the Endangered Species Act for creating a ridiculous obstacle to development. In the end, President Jimmy Carter, already locked in a battle over water resources development projects, signed "with regret" a public works appropriations bill that included a provision that effectively exempted the Tellico Dam from environmental laws. The maneuver stood on such shaky legal ground that just twelve hours after Carter's signature, bulldozers were tearing at the habitat of the unique snail darter. The sensitive and sometimes sanctimonious Carter faced a brutal decision that pitted his beliefs against pragmatic politics. The Endangered Species Act might stand in law, but in the reality of everyday political maneuvering, it became another malleable piece of legislation and little more.

The luster came off quality-of-life environmental legislation during the Tellico Dam controversy. The Endangered
Species Act was scheduled to be reauthorized during 1978,
during the middle of the fray. Faced with a changing economic climate and anger from many quarters, Congress followed the public. It reauthorized the bill but weakened it,
adding new, primarily economic requirements to the assessment process. Most of these new provisions limited the ways
that the biological factors built into the initial bill could halt
federal projects. While to say the bill was gutted would over-
state the case, it did emerge as weaker protection. The use of
the Endangered Species Act at Tellico Dam and the backlash
against it resulted in fewer protections in law for endangered
species. This shift had taken only five years, from 1973, when
the bill was authorized, to 1978, when Congress wavered on
its renewal.

The largely uninhabited state of Nevada had rarely been a catalyst for change in American history, but in the late 1970s it
came to the fore in environmental policy. The "Sagebrush Rebellion," heir to a long tradition that argued for local control
of federal lands and in some cases for returning their jurisdiction to the states in which they were located, struck a chord in
the West and elsewhere in the nation. Articulating an updated
version of states' rights just fifteen years after federal examin-
ers had been sent to the South to assure the voting rights of
African Americans, the Sagebrush rebels advocated local government as the most—and sometimes only—important form
of democracy.
  This philosophy was scarcely new, but it was a challenge to
the way the United States had operated since the end of the
Civil War. That war had been about the concept of union as
much as the issue of slavery; its aftermath had reaffirmed the
federal system in the United States. Although federal author-

ity suffered numerous attacks, especially regarding civil rights, throughout the late nineteenth century and the first half of the twentieth, federal land went unquestioned. Despite the anti-authoritarian cast of the 1960s, even that tumultuous decade saw the expansion and use of federal power to protect land from development rather than allow it to move from national to local hands. In this context the Sagebrush Rebellion seemed anachronistic, a relic of an earlier America.

Larger trends in American society did little to dissuade rural Nevadans, threatened also by the changing economic climate. Early in the 1970s the Select Committee on Public Lands of the Nevada legislature explored the transfer of federal lands to the state after complaints from Nevada ranchers who felt threatened by the Bureau of Land Management. A movement for transfer gathered momentum, and its leaders challenged a number of federal statutes they believed infringed upon their rights. The Sagebrush rebels demanded restructured relations between state and federal governments, and in the view of political leaders such as Senator Barry Goldwater of Arizona and John L. Harmer, lieutenant governor of California under Ronald Reagan, the rebels made valid points. States *should* have more control over what went on within their boundaries, Goldwater and many like him believed. From its inception, the Sagebrush Rebellion presented a genuine challenge to the environmental movement, which depended heavily on federal legislation and the federal bureaucracy.

The idea of "culture and custom," that time-honored patterns of behavior on public land conveyed de facto ownership to longtime users, underpinned the Sagebrush Rebellion. Scarcely different from squatters' rights, this idea lacked a statutory basis. States such as Nevada had given up their public lands as a condition of statehood, and many Western states had never even owned the land they targeted for transfer.

Typically these lands were in the public domain; they were not local land, as Sagebrush rebels liked to insist. They were merely "locally located," proximate to people who had made long use of them under federal terms. Lands controlled by the Bureau of Land Management (BLM), which were the target of most of the appropriation strategy, were those that the agency had received largely because the government could not find anyone to take them. Despite this apparently sensible federal jurisdiction, the Sagebrush Rebellion spoke to deep-seated fears: the emphasis on individual rights during the 1960s; the growing distrust of government in general and the federal government in particular; and disgust with widespread environmental regulations. Westerners self-righteously believed they suffered under a powerful federal lash. The rebels' strident cries reminded the nation of the fears of rural Americans generally, and many who found inspiration in the romantic mythology of the American West offered at least tacit support.

Western legislatures fueled the Sagebrush Rebellion. In 1979 Nevada passed legislation that targeted BLM holdings in Nevada for transfer to state hands, asserted state control of mineral rights and surface access, advocated a multiple-use perspective for management, and protected existing leases made by individuals with the federal government. Other Western politicians embraced the action. Senator Orrin Hatch of Utah introduced a similar bill in the United States Senate in 1979 and became one of the leaders of the revolt, and senators such as Dennis DeConcini and Barry Goldwater of Arizona, Alan Simpson and Malcolm Wallop of Wyoming, Paul Laxalt and Howard Cannon of Nevada, and Jake Garn of Utah joined in. Archconservatives Ted Stevens of Alaska, Jesse Helms of North Carolina, and Richard Jepsen of Iowa also added their names to a long list of Senate supporters.

The Sagebrush Rebellion reshaped nineteenth-century

Western protest in contemporary terms. Proponents of land transfer felt that the federal government controlled the Western economy by controlling too much land in Western states, and that the time had come to end that dominance. New federal legislation added a further twist to their objections. They regarded the Federal Land Policy and Management Act of 1976 (FLPMA), which specified federal land management in perpetuity, as unconstitutional. From the perspective of the rebels, that law made Western states unequal when compared to the original thirteen colonies and Texas, all of which retained control of the land within their borders when they were admitted to the Union. The shift to the constitutional tactic, different from the West's usual petulant posturing, was an important step for those who battled for the extension of states' rights.

The 1980 campaign year became the high-water mark of the Sagebrush Rebellion. Not only did Ronald Reagan, an honorary Sagebrush rebel himself, trounce the incumbent Jimmy Carter for the presidency, but Wyoming, Utah, and New Mexico followed Nevada with bills that claimed sovereignty over BLM lands within state boundaries. Wyoming claimed national forest land as well as that managed by BLM. Arizona joined the rebellion when a general referendum overrode Governor Bruce Babbitt's veto of Sagebrush legislation. Governors Jerry Brown of California and Richard Lamm of Colorado vetoed similar bills; in Washington State one measure passed the legislature but was voided by a 60 percent "no" vote in a referendum. Sagebrush Rebellion bills went down to defeat in Montana, Idaho, and Oregon, but by now the movement had real momentum. Powerful senators from Western states who opposed it fell to election defeat. Frank Church, a longtime senator from Idaho and a staunch advocate of bipartisan conservation and environmentalism, lost to Representative Steve Symms, one of the revolt's loudest voices. The Sagebrush Rebellion attracted wide support in many Western states: opponents of federal power and jurisdiction, libertarians and other free-market advocates, and a range of other interests from the fringes of the political left and right across the nation.

The rebels tapped a reservoir of distaste for twentieth-century change, including the ideas of conservation and environmentalism. In the West, rural voters wielded disproportionate power. Rural leaders controlled numerous state legislatures, and they sought to use political power to restore a cultural and economic agenda that reflected nineteenth-century ideas—when cattle, sheep, and mining interests dominated many Western states—more than those of the twentieth. Yet their successes in 1979 and 1980 masked significant problems. Ranchers no longer represented the increasingly urban and suburban West. Western suburbanites had only mythic sympathy for this reconceived vision of states' rights. Still, when President-elect Ronald Reagan expressed his support—a telegram with the powerful words: "I renew my pledge to work toward a sagebrush solution"—to the second conference of the League for the Advancement of States' Equal Rights in November 1980, Sagebrush rebels could believe they stood in the vanguard of a new—if also old—American movement.

With the appointment of attorney James Watt as Secretary of the Interior, Reagan's support translated into immediate action. A staunch advocate of free-market capitalism and a veteran of more than two decades on the losing side of the environmental wars, Watt planned an all-out assault on the reigning value system. He opposed a comprehensive federal land policy enshrined in law, challenged limits on the development of natural resources, and attacked not only the environmental movement but the laws that underpinned it. A

Wyoming native, the bespectacled and bald Watt was just over 6 feet, 5 inches tall; cartoon caricatures of the man made him seem physically small, but in person he was imposing. He believed in the traditional individualistic ethic of the West, and he made a career of the awkward combination of spouting anti-government rhetoric while accepting ranching subsidies and other federal largesse. In this he was typical of many in the rural West. Watt planned to give the nation's resources to those he called "the people," not the effete elite he believed had controlled them since the Echo Park Dam controversy.

From the day he took office, it was clear that Watt's Department of the Interior would differ from its predecessors. The new secretary seemed to have no respect for the law as it was written, substituting his administrative discretion for statute in a range of circumstances. He announced that the shallows along the scenic northern and central California coasts would be open to offshore oil drilling, something that sent the many powerful and influential people who remembered the Santa Barbara spill into paroxysms of rage. He followed by declaring a moratorium on the acquisition of new land for national parks, enraging yet another constituency. But his agenda was clear. Instead of the values toward which every secretary of the interior since World War II had at least nodded, Watt blatantly favored development. "I will err on the side of public use versus preservation," he defined his philosophy for a March 1981 conference on park concessionaires. "There are people who want to bring their motorcycles and snowmobiles right into the middle of Yellowstone National Park," some claim he told a group of Park Service employees, "and our job is to make sure they *can.*"

Watt's ascendancy drew loud cheers from members of the Sagebrush Rebellion. They could believe their day had come after what seemed an interminable wait. Environmental groups had long enjoyed an easy camaraderie with power. Beginning in the aftermath of Echo Park, a bipartisan coalition of elected officials had regarded all kinds of federal projects as a way to help their constituents. Representative Wayne Aspinall of Colorado, Senator Alan Bible of Nevada, Senator Clinton P. Anderson of New Mexico, Representative Phillip Burton of California, Representative Winfield S. Denton of Indiana, Representative Joe Skubitz of Kansas, and Representative John Sieberling of Ohio routinely promoted dams, roads, and other projects that offered recreational options along with development possibilities. Some supported national parks and other preservation-oriented projects as well. Their success rested on a bipartisan view of the federal government as an active and dominant force. Ronald Reagan ran against the perception, providing the reason why his victory so heartened the Sagebrush Rebellion.

The Reagan administration's emphasis on replacing federal action with state and local government created hostility for bipartisan environmentalism. A bomb-thrower in the best tradition, Watt became the architect of its demise. He served as the point man for a return to earlier ideas about making national policy concur with local standards. By focusing on the larger public that environmentalists had begun to take for granted, Watt fractured existing alliances and turned old allies against one another. A new day had begun, one in which environmentalists had to grapple on even terms with proponents of development.

Watt also exemplified the shift to the political right in the Republican party after Watergate. The Nelson Rockefeller wing of the party, the liberal Republicans, were the biggest losers in the Watergate scandal. Their constituency fled the Grand Old Party, leaving the well-established centrist Republicans in a party that did not value them. A new group, culturally displaced in a changing nation and heavily Southern at first, replaced the liberals and took control of the party apparatus. They moved the Republican party far to the right; the core of Ronald Reagan's support was as suspicious of centrist Republicans as it was of Democrats. During the campaign, Reagan's aides trotted out prominent Republicans with outstanding environmental credentials, such as former EPA directors Russell Train and William Ruckelshaus and former Assistant Secretary of the Interior Nathaniel P. Reed; but once in office, Watt and his friends had free reign. Their choices reflected both the agenda of the new administration and the new face of the Republican party.

With the full support of the Reagan administration, Watt tried to draw a line that defined environmentalism out of the American mainstream and made its advocates extremists. He underestimated the strength of support for environmentalism as he devised a strategy to alter forever Department of the Interior management policies. He ordered most of the departmental management regulations rewritten, smugly contending that his decision would be permanent because no successor would "have the determination I do." Relying on Solicitor William Coldiron, the top legal official in the Department of the Interior and a former attorney for the Montana Power Company, Watt set out to make federal resources accessible to anyone who wanted them, whether or not statute prohibited their development.

The declining economy made Watt's approach more attractive to business interests than it might have been under other circumstances. The end of the Vietnam War and the OPEC oil embargo in 1974 precipitated a drop in the value of hourly wages while the nation's physical plant grew old and American management stagnated. By the time Reagan took office, commercial interest rates of more than 20 percent curtailed investment, and manufacturing jobs were disappearing at a rate noticed even in popular music—when Bruce Springsteen sang, "Foreman says these jobs are going and they ain't coming back," he revealed greater acuity than some policymakers. By the early 1980s America was in a full-fledged recession. When timber, mining, and grazing industry representatives sought access to government-controlled resources in the early 1980s, they did so out of a sense of necessity that reflected both the importance of federal holdings and a fundamental lack of imagination in the private sector.

The situation seemed to pit jobs against the environment in the starkest of terms, but the results showed far more suppleness on the part of Americans. The changing economy primarily hurt industrial, blue-collar work into the early eighties, but by the middle of the decade government workers and corporate middle management were also feeling its effects. Even when business framed the choice as being between growth and environmental protection, countless Americans regarded Watt's Department of the Interior as the real threat to their interests. They simply did not believe that the choices they faced were as absolute as Watt and other Reagan administration officials described them. Mainstream environmental organizations experienced remarkable growth in membership as a direct consequence of Watt's policies. Between 1977 and 1980 the Sierra Club added only 3,000 members to reach a total of 181,000. In 1983 it topped 346,000. The Wilderness Society experienced even greater percentage growth—48,000 members in 1979, and 100,000 four years later; by 1989, 333,000 people belonged to the organization, and in 1995 membership pushed 600,000. Even less politically active organizations such as the Audubon Society enjoyed unprecedented growth. Its 300,000 membership in 1979 grew to 500,000 in 1983. This broad support, especially during a recession, revealed much more than opposition to the policies of the Reagan administration. It also showed how completely Americans embraced the concept of environmentalism and how closely it related to their sense of the quality of their life.

The response showed a new maturity for American environmentalism, a resilience and an ability to reach into a deep well of public support to combat powerful adversaries. Americans knew what they wanted, and on environmental issues their goals were not those of Watt and the Reagan administration. The increasing public disdain for government helped. It was easy to distrust leadership anyway, and the public pronouncements of Watt, which often sounded poorly thought out and strident, inspired little respect. Environmentalists fashioned a sharp attack on power even as the compromise mechanisms of the 1970s seemed less likely to succeed.

In the 1970s environmentalists had begun to divide into more specialized groups; the Reagan-era assault on environmentalism promoted this trend. The Sierra Club, the primary national group since the turn of the century, maintained a broad-based center. But by the 1980s more than a hundred major conservation and environmental groups competed for dollars and support. Some, such as the Natural Resources Defense Council (NRDC), experienced spectacular growth in the eighties. Its appeal to the middle class was its willingness to litigate. Groups such as the more staid National Wildlife Federation lost membership between 1979 and 1983, presumably to more activist organizations. Environmental groups were no longer of a piece. Instead they represented a broad spectrum of views, from discussion of litigation and even to direct action. Centrist organizations such as the Sierra Club, the Audubon Society, and the National Parks and Conservation Association held the middle. NRDC and similar organizations spent their time in court, and direct action remained the province of Greenpeace, founded in 1972, and Earth First!

The first truly ecologically radical environmental group, Earth First! carried the banner of anti-establishment direct action. Its slogan, "No compromise in defense of Mother Earth," reflected many of the ideas of the sixties in a new format. Using the tactics of the civil rights movement and student protests, the organizations believed in an approach to preservation that owed much to the noted environmental author and iconoclast Edward Abbey and his 1975 book *The Monkey Wrench Gang*. They chained themselves to trees, blocked bulldozers, and even spiked trees with long nails and marked them, forcing timber companies to abandon plans to cut the trees for fear of injury to workers. "Monkey wrenching," as spiking and other versions of "ecotage"—ecological sabotage—were labeled, made confrontation in the wilderness as much a psychological factor in the battle for the environment as it had been for the mountain men of the early nineteenth century. On March 31, 1981, Earth First! appeared on the national scene, unfurling a black plastic tarpaulin with a three-hundred-foot crack painted on it, over the Glen Canyon Dam, ever the symbol of outrage for environmentalists. "Earth First!" shouted Abbey from the walkway atop the dam. "Free the Colorado [River]!" Guerrilla theater, an aggressive posture, and the willingness to do anything to protect wilderness characterized the organization from its outset.

Earth First! began when co-founder Dave Foreman, a former employee of the Wilderness Society, looked at the Forest Service's handling of wilderness and felt disgusted. In 1979 the agency had recommended only fifteen million of the eighty million roadless acres on national forest land for wilderness status, and wilderness advocates failed to compel the agency to rethink its perspective. After what Foreman regarded as a stunning defeat, he left Washington, D.C., and the Wilderness Society and returned to his forte, grassroots organizing. He believed that the environmental movement had lost touch with its roots and his values. Its moderate tone seemed destined to fail as increasingly zealous and powerful opponents bashed wilderness protection. "We looked like statesmen,"

Foreman recalled. "They won." So Foreman and a cadre of activists, including Howie Wolke, a former Friends of the Earth worker; Susan Morgan, former educational director for the Wilderness Society; Bart Koehler, also from the Wilderness Society; Mike Roselle, the most radical leftist of the group; and others disgruntled with the mainstream formed the new organization.

With Watt in office and the Sagebrush Rebellion under way, Foreman and Earth First! seemed a reasonable counterweight to extreme forces on the other side. Those who believed environmentalism could remain within the system and succeed with compromise found their numbers diminishing. Although insiders negotiating compromises had been responsible for most of the victories of conservation and environmentalism, the strategy seemed increasingly archaic. Negotiating with Watt and others like him was almost impossible. It was as if the premises of the two sides simply did not intersect.

Earth First! anchored the left wing of environmentalism, making the center more palatable to die-hard opponents such as Watt. Instead of Foreman of Earth First! or even Abbey, politicians, agency officials, and resource users could sit down with people such as Doug Scott, the consummate Sierra Club negotiator, and the better-dressed crowd from the Wilderness Society or the National Parks and Conservation Association. Even Watt could have civil discussions with some environmentalists, it seemed, especially if the alternative was having people whom the secretary regarded as long-haired crazies running around his woods. Although Earth First! alone might embarrass the mainstream, having a spectrum of environmental groups provided more consistent success than any single narrow approach. From a strategic position, despite all the trouble Earth First! caused for environmental organizations, its presence strengthened their ability to negotiate with business and industry. Foreman's fringe became a valuable part of an expanding repertoire.

While the Reagan administration assumed it had a voters' mandate for its policies, its popularity did not stretch to the environment. White America, reeling from the cultural changes of the sixties and the economic decline of the seventies, was enthusiastic about Reagan's "Morning in America." But when it came to harvesting timber, destroying watersheds and rivers, and polluting the skies, Americans—even those who made their living from natural resources—remained tied to their mythic vision of a pristine continent. They too embraced the quality-of-life movement. They wanted clear skies *and* high-paying blue-collar jobs, and time and again they opposed rapacious development of the resources they depended on for their living. Even the timber workers of northern California, facing the closing of plywood mills and the loss of timber industry jobs to workers overseas, recognized that the industry was even more culpable than the nearby Redwood National Park they often blamed for their predicament. America had always thought of itself as "nature's nation." Its response in the face of trying circumstances confirmed that self-image.

Despite Reagan's enormous popularity, his appointees failed to reflect public opinion on environmental questions. The administration was loaded with people from the industries that Americans expected their government to regulate. Reagan's EPA chief had been hired direct from the chemical industry, one of the most consistent polluters of land and water. Power companies and extractive industries laced the Department of the Interior. Sensing the ways in which many of these officials were captives of specific constituencies, environmentalists worked to ensure that their policy decisions received public scrutiny. The foolish-sounding rationalizations that often accompanied official pronouncements became one of the few public relations failures of the Reagan administration. Watt's blustery rhetoric made him the subject of ridicule, and other Reagan administration officials, especially EPA chief Anne Gorsuch Burford and her husband, BLM head Robert Burford, appeared even more preposterous. Reagan's charisma muted public resentment, but his department heads and agency leaders and representatives often damaged the very causes they sought to help.

Watt was more out of step with the public than any Reagan-era bureau chief, and his penchant for speaking his mind made him a target. His views inspired the ire of environmentalists and the concern of nearly everyone else. During the confirmation hearings on his appointment, Watt told Congress that long-term planning was futile because the return of the Messiah was imminent. Senators scratched their heads in confusion and dismay; the public thought him a crank. When the courts ruled repeatedly that Watt's rule changes exceeded his authority, he lost credibility. "I Know Watt's Wrong" graced the bumpers of cars and trucks across the nation. The teeming war chests of environmental organizations demonstrated the secretary's unpopularity and brought to an end the Sagebrush Rebellion's moment in the sun.

By 1983 Watt was the least popular member of the administration, and his odd and insulting manner soon forced him from office. That year he noted that the membership of a Department of the Interior advisory board consisted of "a black . . . a woman, two Jews, and a cripple. And we have talent." This disparaging and basically nasty statement offended many, even a number of Watt's strongest supporters. He resigned soon after, his environmental revolution in tatters. Watt posed a genuine threat to the bipartisan consensus that supported the environmental movement, but he lacked both the tact and skill to fracture existing relationships and drive a permanent wedge between allies. His successes were temporary. Instead Watt taught the environmental movement how to work outside the system, honing its organizing and public relations skills. Watt raised the stakes in environmental politics, but he could not hold the territory he captured. Those who agreed with him were left well funded by industry but on the margins of American culture.

By the mid-1980s a series of intellectually related but largely independent movements fed off the growing fear of loss that permeated middle-class white America. For most working-class Americans, in industry or natural resources extraction, life had grown meaner since the 1960s. Not only had job opportunities at good wages in their industries diminished with few commensurate replacements, but the cultural climate seemed to blame *them* for their predicament. In a world of affirmative action and endangered species protection, who looked out for the working class? Disaffection spread so widely among the socio-economic middle of the country, the old New Deal coalition, that Ronald Reagan's trouncing of Walter Mondale in the 1984 presidential election came to be called "the revenge of the white male."

Beyond the perimeters of general dissatisfaction, a series of groups promoted a more radical ideology: that the time had come to turn the clock back to an earlier America, where individuals were white and Christian and did as they pleased. Some of the dimensions of this movement were radical, millennial, and violent. The actions of the Silent Brotherhood, which robbed banks and in 1984 murdered Denver radio personality Alan Berg to promote its idea of a white nation in the inland Northwest, and the 1995 bombing of the Alfred P. Murrah Federal Building in Oklahoma City, were the most extreme examples.

Equally radical from a political perspective but tamer in its approach was the property rights movement. Reflecting the values of the Sagebrush Rebellion, it directed much of its ire at the federal government and especially at environmental regulations. Property rights advocates echoed a long-standing American axiom: an individual's property was his to do with as he pleased, and damn the consequences. While in general this point of view held true in American history, the power of eminent domain, the right of the state to take individual property for the common good as long as the owner was fairly compensated, was well established in English common law and continued in the United States. After 1945, environmental regulations encroached upon individual rights in small ways. From the Antiquities Act of 1906 to the Endangered Species Act, laws provided for situations where national interest far exceeded individual rights in environmental questions. The property rights movements rejected any notion of the common good, however, regarding individual property as sacrosanct in all settings.

Right-wing theory and money widely supported this concept. The Heritage Foundation (a Washington, D.C., think tank that set the agenda for the Reagan administration), the CATO Institute, the National Rifle Association (NRA), and similar groups advocated individuality over community. While much of this support went to legitimate groups with political objectives that operated within the mainstream of American society, a reasonable portion supported the lunatic fringe. Somewhere in between arose the Wise Use movement, a well-financed right-wing effort that used corporate funding to fashion a phony grassroots initiative in an attempt to derail the environmental movement.

Wise Use grew out of the fusion of the ideas of two individuals, Alan Gottlieb and Ron Arnold, who met when Gottlieb read the jacket flap of Arnold's book, *At the Eye of the Storm:*

James Watt and the Environmentalists, and discovered that they both lived in Seattle. Gottlieb, a New Right activist who grew up in a liberal Jewish New York family, attended the University of Tennessee, became a conservative after reading Barry Goldwater, and converted to Catholicism. He was one of the direct-mail gurus of right-wing causes. By the 1980s he had settled in Seattle, where he established Liberty Park, a business park financed by nonprofit foundations owned by Gottlieb but titled to himself and his wife. At Liberty Park, Gottlieb's Center for the Defense of Free Enterprise (CDFE) and his Second Amendment Foundation kept their headquarters along with the offices of a range of anti-tax, anti-abortion, and other conservative groups. Sporting a prophetlike long white beard, Ron Arnold was hired as CDFE's executive vice president in 1984. A native of Texas who had once been a member of the Sierra Club, he claimed to have become disgruntled by what he alleged was a smear campaign against Weyerhaueser timber operations. Others who were present suggest that Arnold fabricated the events, but beginning about 1970 Arnold changed sides and embarked on an all-out assault on environmental groups, protected lands, and environmentalism in general. His commentary was often bombastic. "The National Park Service," he once said of the most popular federal agency, "is an empire designed to eliminate all private property in the United States."

Espousing the philosophy that the only way to defeat one social movement is with another, Arnold began the Wise Use movement. In many ways it was a direct response to environmentalism, an attempt to turn the huge, largely passive number of Americans who defined environmentalism as a secular religion against their own beliefs. Arnold embraced the same tactics as the movement he scorned, fashioning anti-environmentalism as in the best interests of all and against extremists, this time a self-described elite rather than corporate leaders. Tying closely into the idea of deregulation that was one of the buzzwords of the Reagan era, Arnold and his supporters sought to use the proliferation of regulations as a way to provoke the growing disaffection of the old middle class.

In a time when blue-collar workers were losing their jobs, occasionally as a result of environmental action, this strategy enjoyed a certain appeal. But Wise Use depended on corporate largesse to a much greater degree than did pro-environmental groups, calling into question Arnold's claim to be the initiator of a grassroots movement. A clearly defined constituency did emerge: it included a small cadre of scientists who regarded environmentalism as part of an anti-human movement; beneficiaries of industrial and agricultural access to lands and water at below-market costs; and property rights advocates who saw their profits threatened by laws that protected wetlands, endangered species, wild and scenic rivers, or other natural resources. Surprisingly the group made little headway with off-road vehicle advocates or snowmobilers. Another seemingly natural constituency, hunters, possessed of the conservation ethic that even television hunting and fishing shows promote, generally shied away as well.

Wise Use had a dirty underbelly, a long list of attacks on environmentalists and those who protested pollution and other excesses by industry. Arnold's rhetoric contributed to the acerbic climate: "We are engaged in a holy war against the new pagans," he said. Some environmentalists who opposed Wise Use had their homes destroyed; some were attacked—at least one was knifed and another raped. In 1993 American Indian environmentalist Leroy Jackson died under mysterious circumstances just days before he was to testify about clearcutting on the Navajo Reservation. His friends believe he was murdered. "Death threats come with the territory these days,"

remarked Andy Kerr of the Oregon Natural Resources Council in a sad testimony to the obvious degeneration of American
cultural and political dialogue.

Opposition to environmentalism may have served as an ex-
cuse for psychopathic violence, but many stood within the law
as they battled the legal and institutional revolution that
environmentalism had become. These sentiments were particularly potent in the West, where "culture and custom" arguments gave longtime private lessees de facto ownership of
public land. Especially in cases of land with great recreational
value, urban constituencies felt strong ties to rural land and
often regarded it as their own. Although sympathetic to the
contentions of rural people, the people of the ever-spreading
Western suburbs wanted to hunt, fish, and camp without pay-
ing a fortune for the privilege. The battle lines were clear:
urban recreation versus rural grazing and timber cutting.

Rural Nevada became the flashpoint for this issue. Nye
County, the rural and barely inhabited county northwest of
Las Vegas, became the center of a controversy between the
County Movement, an arm of the property rights movement,
and the federal government. On July 4, 1993, with the United
States Constitution in his pocket, Nye County Commissioner
Richard Carver drove a bulldozer at a Forest Service ranger as
he opened a dirt road that had been closed by the Forest Service. Carver believed that the federal government had no
rights within Nevada or any other state, a position that the
Nevada legislature and governor did not share. When challenged, Carver tapped his shirt pocket and invoked the Constitution.

Nye County typified places where the Wise Use movement
easily found sympathy. Its few people had deep roots in the region, and most thought of themselves as independent of larger
forces in American society. This posture was pure fiction.

Most worked for the federal government, either at the Nevada Test Site or at the proposed high-level nuclear waste dump at Yucca Mountain. Federal money filled the county's coffers, but a small minority of ranchers wielded autocratic power there. Carver, a rancher, set himself up as the leader. He felt oppressed by what he regarded as an unjust federal government. He was just folk, he often contended, trying to make a living from a harsh land.

Violence was never far from the Wise Use movement. In 1995, before the Oklahoma bombing, the Forest Service office in Nevada's capital, Carson City, about 250 miles northwest of Nye County, became a target: a bomb exploded outside the building. In August, Forest Service District Director Guy Pence's van blew up in his driveway while his wife and daughters were in the house. One child stepped into the house moments before the blast. Although the Nye County Commission offered a $100,000 reward in an effort to find the perpetrator, anti-government rhetoric had clearly created the climate in which the attack occurred. Pence rejected the veiled apology, observing that a county that claimed federal lands in Nevada did not exist had no business offering money received from the federal government (the primary source of revenue in Nye County) to wash its hands of the violence it inspired. The Nye County commissioners were insulted and withdrew their offer. One remarked that Pence's "posturing encourages violence against federal bureaucrats."

Such a pronouncement revealed the disingenuousness at the heart of the local control movement. Carver's Constitution protected his privilege. He used the ideals of American society as a way to block change, to transform law into a tool for people who above all owned property. An attempt to change statute by implicit force, the County movement wanted to be rid of any level of government beyond its own. It was a version of the nullification that Southern states had threatened against civil rights, but the strategy was exposed when Nye County claimed the authority to accept nuclear waste in the county while the State of Nevada fought it. The state legislature angrily asserted its authority, but Nye County made its point: it depended on state and federal government for the dollars that built its roads and schools, but the pipeline was to run only one way. Rural counties would do as they pleased unless the state stopped them. Rural communities no longer felt part of any larger dimension of community, nor did locals believe laws and strictures applied to them. If allowed to stand, this idea was a threat to the majority-rule principle that had governed the United States for more than two hundred years.

The property rights movement was also about larger issues, chief among them the return to individualism, always a mythic dimension of American life. Nostalgia for a fictitious moment in the American past, when the "little guy" counted, became widespread in the aftermath of the Microchip Revolution, every bit as great a transformation as the Industrial Revolution. As hundreds of thousands of factory workers and corporate managers found themselves out of work throughout the seventies and eighties, and unable to replace their high wages at new employment, the claim of good old American self-reliance, dating at least as far back as Ralph Waldo Emerson, seemed a salve for psychic wounds.

Environmentalism in its post-1970s form was the antithesis of that independence. It suggested a finite world, still a frightening prospect for Americans a hundred years after the 1890 Census. It advocated a communal approach to all things: nature, human endeavor, and social interaction. It also promoted restraint, a decidedly un-American idea. As such it became a target for those frustrated by change and by the loss of their position and prerogative. The excesses of environmentalists also contributed to the backlash. Before environmentalism could claim complete loyalty from the American public, it had to answer broader questions than those merely of the outdoors.

8

A New Environmentalism

As the American economy declined in the 1970s and early 1980s, a new urban-oriented environmentalism found its voice while support for wilderness and species preservation seemed less urgent. Issues still concerned quality of life, but now they were more closely related to questions of public health. These questions galvanized a broad segment of the public, well beyond those groups who cared for endangered species and wilderness. Opposed to nuclear power and toxic waste, these new advocates came from all walks of American life. They were as likely to be nuclear physicists as housewives, African American as patrician-class whites. Faced with real threats to things they valued, they spoke out loudly—for protection, but not necessarily for the kind of environmentalism promoted by the Sierra Club and similar organizations.

Nuclear power became a paramount issue, drawing opposition across class and racial lines. The military uses of nuclear power were secretive, and across the nation people looked at fences that concealed nuclear activity and worried. For years many of them had had reason for genuine concern. When the wind had blown fallout from an atomic explosion on the Nevada Test Site to the north and east in the late 1950s, some of the ranchers around Baker, Nevada, soon found men in protective suits roaming the region. Geiger counters went "hot," recording levels of radiation off the scale of measurement. Sheep and cattle died mysteriously. No one ever explained what had happened to the people who lived in these communities, but as some of them sickened with unusual cancers, their distrust of government activity grew. As the number of such cases became better known, a public groundswell against the construction of nuclear power plants and the testing of nuclear materials arose.

The opposition to nuclear power gained momentum very quickly in 1970s America. Initially it began as opposition to the heat generated by nuclear power, not its radioactive releases, contaminated waste, or the prospects of an accident. The subsequent battle focused on control of the standards governing the release of radioactive by-products. The Atomic Energy Commission (AEC) and various states fought over who should set these standards. These fights created the context for more comprehensive attacks on civilian nuclear power. By the early 1970s the prospect of a nuclear accident of serious proportions also frightened nuclear physicists and engineers. The Union of Concerned Scientists, made up of many of the leading scientists of the era, and anti-nuclear—or "anti-nuke," as they came to be called—groups led the charge. Nuclear power plants under construction were besieged. Protesters blocked access to the Diablo Canyon reactor, astride the San Andreas fault in California; the Shoreham plant on Long Island, New York, where there was no adequate evacuation plan for the residents of Long Island in case of an emergency; and the Seabrook plant in New Hampshire, among many others. Their actions attracted first the curiosity of the public and then its respect, and by the mid-seventies a faultline divided the nation on the question of nuclear power.

This line cut different ways. In one sense it pitted belief in the infinite capability of human beings against those who believed the world was finite. Proponents of nuclear energy believed that technological innovation was a step toward creating new opportunities, economic and otherwise, for the human race. Cornucopian economists, whose most basic belief could be described as "more is better in all circumstances," were among those who argued this case. Opposing them were those who believed that nuclear technology and its application were a Pandora's box. Its promise of cheap, infinite, and, from the standpoint of conventional pollution, clean fuel was a trap that involved too much risk for the benefits it offered. It had the added disadvantage of promising infinite power in an age sensitized to limits. The two sides represented a larger conflict of values in American society, well beyond the power of science to solve. Neither side accepted the other's premises, and compromise was impossible. Resolution became a function of politics.

The larger question nuclear power asked was: what kind of risks might a democratic society bear to assure sufficient prosperity and realize true democracy? Coal-fired power sources created air pollution and haze, spewing millions of tons of particulate matter into the air. These were an ongoing nuisance, but the limits of their ability to harm were quite apparent. Nuclear power offered an alternative, and when its plants worked properly it succeeded beyond anyone's wildest expectations. But a cloud hung over the nuclear industry, as much a result of military activity as anything the civilian industry had done, and Americans who coveted the clean air that nuclear power produced also feared the consequences of its embrace. Just one accident, one explosion, could forever mar not only the skies but the land as well. Popular sentiment moved away from nuclear power, and American politicians picked up the signal from their constituents. After 1974, no new nuclear plant construction reached completion.

By the end of the 1970s, opposition to nuclear power had become a widespread phenomenon that even entered American
popular culture. In 1978 a film called *The China Syndrome*
demonstrated how Americans felt about nuclear power. In it
Jane Fonda plays a reporter who stumbles onto a nuclear reactor accident in California. Officials at the plant try to cover up
the incident that ends in the death—presumably by murder—
of the whistle-blower. A catastrophe is only avoided by the
heroine's quick thinking. Although the film can be read as an
indictment of television news as well as the nuclear power industry, most who saw it shivered in their seats and hoped that
this movie would never become reality.

But life imitated art on March 28, 1979, when the core of
Unit 2 of the Metropolitan Edison Company's nuclear reactor
on Three Mile Island in Pennsylvania, outside of Harrisburg,
went critical and caused a partial meltdown. A simple mechanical function shut down the reactor. Water pumps cooled
the system, but when a pressure relief valve opened, allowing
water and steam to escape into the reactor's containment system, the cooling liquid was diverted away from the 100-ton
uranium fuel core. A water-level gauge stuck; workers did not
notice, and for two hours the relief valve remained open. In
that time more than 1 million gallons of water were pumped
away from the core, leaving its top half dry and scorching hot.
Human error complicated matters. Workers misunderstood
the problem, left the valve open, and shut off an emergency
cooling system that might have brought the reactor temperature down. Instead it exceeded 5,000 degrees Fahrenheit,
melting the top half of the core. Two hours after the malfunc-
tion, operators released a flood of cooling water in the reactor,
shattering the remainder of the core.

The public sensed immediate danger in the situation at the
reactor. Panic ensued as word of the mishap spread. The plant

released radioactive steam into the atmosphere on at least two occasions as part of its effort to cool the core. More than twelve hours after the initial shutdown, the reactor remained at more than 550 degrees Fahrenheit. Radiation leaks continued, and a terrified public watched in dismay, wondering whether to flee. Schools closed, and radio and television broadcasts urged people not to venture outside. With the ongoing release of radiation into the environment, Pennsylvania Governor Richard Thornburgh ordered pregnant women and children evacuated. If anything, this accelerated the panic. False reports of uncontrolled radiation releases compelled more than 200,000 people to leave the region as quickly as possible. The worst aspect of the transformation to nuclear power became abundantly clear: radiation could not be seen, tasted, or smelled, but its very existence promoted unparalleled terror.

Three Mile Island was headline news, a story to top all stories. It led the national television evening news twelve days running; no single event since the assassination of Martin Luther King, Jr., in 1968 had received greater television coverage. Advocates of nuclear power had long sworn that no such thing could happen, but here it was, a situation that took the ordinary to the realm of paralyzing terror. In the end, the amount of radiation released turned out to be insignificant, but the terror and mistrust that the incident inspired were genuine and immense. On the heels of Watergate, and in a time when Americans simply did not place much trust in their government, Three Mile Island demolished the public's last vestiges of confidence in the safety of nuclear power.

Severe accidents with nuclear power both preceded and followed Three Mile Island, but the widespread impact of the Pennsylvania disaster was unparalleled. In 1965 a fire had exposed hundreds of workers at the Rocky Flats Nuclear Weapons Facility; in 1970 the Dresden-2 reactor near Chicago went out of control and released radioactive iodine; in 1973 the drinking water of St. Paul, Minnesota, absorbed 50,000 gallons of untreated nuclear wastewater; in 1977 two maintenance workers at the Pilgrim-1 nuclear plant in Massachusetts entered the wrong room and were exposed to radiation, one of them severely overexposed. The disaster at Church Rock, New Mexico, when 100 million gallons of radioactive water spilled into the Rio Puerco after a tailings dam at the United Nuclear Corporation's mill there breached, attracted less attention than Three Mile Island. Although some have called the July 16, 1979, Church Rock spill "the worst nuclear disaster in American history," its victims were largely Navajo and their sheep. Even the Chernobyl disaster in the Soviet Union in 1986 lacked the resonance of Three Mile Island. Was it because neither Church Rock nor Chernobyl affected ordinary Americans? Navajo people, Soviet citizens, and nuclear plant workers were all somehow apart from the American mainstream. But Three Mile Island, especially on the heels of *The China Syndrome*, struck home.

Even more dangerous and more mysterious than nuclear meltdown was the threat from hazardous waste and solvents stored improperly across the country. Toxic waste predated the beginning of the atomic age, but it seemed, like many similar problems, merely a by-product of progress—a dangerous one, perhaps, but one that had to be endured. Rachel Carson had sounded the alarm on pesticides, leading to the banning of DDT, but ordinary household chemicals continued in wide use, only mildly regulated, and some posed a genuine threat. American life was closely entwined with all kinds of chemicals, from lead-based paint to turpentine, all of which were in everyday use and seemed innocuous. Yet for the average American in an average day, they were far more dangerous than a nuclear accident.

Before *Silent Spring*, the products derived from natural and synthetic chemicals had been regarded as an unmitigated good, a way to control everything from fire ants and mosquitoes, to make paint last longer, glue stick better, or plastic more malleable. Children throughout the South played in the DDT spray from mosquito-control trucks; despite the fact that the danger of lead exposure had been known for more than two thousand years, paint was laced with lead to make it last longer. One of the most prominent brands of the 1920s was "Dutch Boy White Lead Paint," a testimony to the way that the use of chemicals cut both ways. In the 1920s and beyond this paint was prized for its durability. In the 1970s and 1980s, when Dr. Herbert Needleman of the University of Pittsburgh studied the effects of lead-based paint, he found the highest levels of toxicity in the large and graceful older homes that dotted American cities. Once well-maintained by the affluent who had long since left for the suburbs, these cracking, peeling structures, now divided into apartments, had become dens of contamination, especially for the many small children who lived there. Prolonged exposure even to lead dust, a common feature whenever old paint disintegrated, caused diminished brain growth in younger children, leading to the prospect of entire generations permanently intellectually damaged by circumstances beyond their control. Although the use of lead in paint was banned in 1977, as late as the mid-1990s state disclosure laws did not require that sellers of property acknowledge the possibility of lead-based paint. Only in 1995 did the Department of Housing and Urban Development (HUD) issue strictures for lead paint in properties under its jurisdiction.

Common substances were only the tip of the iceberg of potential toxicity. No place in the nation was safe; waste from industrial processes was everywhere, sometimes in safe and appropriate storage, other times in rotting fifty-five-gallon barrels. Often chemicals, solvents, and other toxic materials were simply taken to remote rural locations and dumped or buried. In North Carolina in 1978 a man named Robert Burns and his two sons drove liquid tanker trucks filled with polychlorinated biphenyls (PCBs) from the Ward Transformer Company in Raleigh and emptied their contents along 240 miles of state roads. Even industries that had long sustained communities left a toxic residue in their wake. When the Wagner Electric Company announced plans to close its Hillside Works facility in Wellston, Missouri, in 1981, the impact was more than economic. The company left 4,000 gallons of contaminated oil as well as a legacy of spillage and careless disposal—a typical instance of industrial nonchalance about toxic materials.

The quality-of-life movement and the end of the bargain between workers and their employers over risks and wages encouraged Americans to speak out where before they had held their tongues. As businesses began to abandon their workers, the ties of loyalty were strained and then torn. People who once benefited from industrial work now complained loudly about its consequences. The sprawl of postwar American cities and rapidly increasing land values brought families in often unknowing close proximity to areas that had been used as wastelands or dumps. As farmland turned to neighborhoods, people moved into new homes believing that the land beneath them was as fresh as the paint on their walls. In some circumstances, a fermenting and toxic combination of chemicals lay beneath the ground, spreading into underground water courses where people lived and worked and where their children played.

The ironically named Love Canal, near Niagara Falls, New York, became the first widely known battle between local industry and the public. Before mid-century the Hooker Chemical Company had filled an old canal with a "veritable witches' brew of chemistry, compounds of truly remarkable toxicity," according to reporter Michael Brown of the *Niagara Gazette*. In 1953 the Niagara Falls Board of Education took possession of the tract for a token payment of one dollar and constructed a school. A neighborhood took shape around it, comprised of typical Niagara Falls area people: chemical and industrial plant workers and their families. Nothing seemed to separate Love Canal from thousands of similar developments around the country.

Despite the illusion of typicality, Love Canal was different. It smelled. It oozed. Unusual events occurred. In 1958 three children received burns from chemical residues on the canal surface. Children threw chunks of phosphorus, which they called "fire rocks," against cement; they exploded, sending off a trail of white sparks. During hot weather, fires sometimes erupted for no apparent reason, and small explosions often followed. The persistent odor was considered part of life in an industrialized community—a cost of prosperity. Love Canal was one of thousands of middle-class communities inhabited by first-generation homeowners and tied to the industrial enterprises that put the American Dream within their grasp.

But birth defects were common in Love Canal, and so were unusual illnesses and deafness in children. Youngsters at Love Canal were statistical aberrations. By any measure they far exceeded American norms for the incidence of disease. Adults were also susceptible. Women who lived in the area were diagnosed with a variety of cancers at rates far above the national average. Even pets were not immune. Cats and dogs commonly carried lesions on their skin, and many had bald patches. For all its surface typicality, Love Canal hid real and frightening abnormalities.

As late as the 1970s, Love Canal residents regarded these circumstances as their own personal misfortune, but in fact they sat atop a serious health hazard that was well known to local and state officials. The ailments that were typical in the neighborhood occurred with a frequency so unusual in the population at large that it was clear some external toxin was at work. Local government helped cover up the problem. Well into 1978, the city of Niagara Falls publicly denied it knew of any problem at Love Canal; but as early as 1976, local officials informed the state Department of Environmental Conservation that the neighborhood teemed with subsurface toxins. City officials even held secret meetings with the Hooker Chemical Company, the largest industry in the community, to discuss how to conceal the problem.

A new kind of public activism propelled the story to public attention and compelled both government and industry to address the problems at Love Canal. A persistent campaign by local organizer Lois Gibbs and reporter Michael Brown made the situation a public issue. In October 1977 EPA officials advocated the evacuation of Love Canal. In May 1978 the EPA reported that cancer-causing benzene permeated household air there. Even after the announcement, the county health commissioner and the city manager of Niagara Falls publicly minimized the threat. Hooker Chemical also denied the problem. Only on August 2, 1978, when state health commissioner Dr. Robert Whalen declared Love Canal a "great and imminent peril to the health of the general public," did other public officials address the consequences of the wastes buried there.

Whalen's declaration simultaneously solved problems and caused new ones. It assigned governmental responsibility in a clear way, an advantage for the terrified people at Love Canal. But it also inflamed a highly charged situation. After Whalen spoke, people who thought their health problems were only their own instantly recognized that their lives had been ruined by one of the companies that sustained them. In response, they fiercely attacked Hooker Chemical and local government. Although assured that the state would purchase their homes, individuals had no plans for their departure. They could not go on with their lives in Love Canal, nor did most have the resources simply to leave.

Turmoil ensued. Residents did not know whom they could trust, and with the bizarre decision to locate the crisis center in the elementary school atop the dump, they did not even know if they were safe when they went there to seek help. They packed the school, waiting for the blood test that would show—hope beyond hope for most—that they were lucky, clean of chemical contamination. Children cried; their mothers tried to comfort them without letting their own pain and fear show through. No one went to work. They feared being unable to return if the entire area were quarantined. Families nearly came to blows: should they stay or should they leave? No one knew. Was the damage to themselves and their children already done, they asked, or would waiting a few more days make everything worse? For everyone involved, it was a terrible time, full of fear, anger, and unbelievable anxiety.

The terror ended while Love Canal awaited the visit of New York Governor Hugh Carey on August 7. President Jimmy Carter declared the Hooker Chemical dump site a national emergency, and the people of Love Canal breathed a little easier. Carey promised that the state would purchase all the affected homes at fair market value. Evacuation followed, with a remediation program at a cost of more than $30 million, and within a year the immediate area stabilized. By the following spring, 237 families had been relocated. A green, eight-foot-high chain-link fence soon surrounded the six-square-block section believed to be the most contaminated. The neighborhood stood in silent testimony to the cost of industrial progress.

Love Canal proved to be the first of a seemingly endless series of revelations about the toxicity of progress. They came in waves, not incidentally tied to the changing American workplace. The decline of the traditional industrial economy and its cost in the loyalty—and silence—of employees paralleled the disappointment Americans felt in the leadership of their society. The distrust of people in power, depicted as common sense in music, film, and nearly every other medium, and the rise in toxic-related ailments, often a result of the average twenty-year lag between exposure and the appearance of many forms of cancer, all spelled trouble for American industry. Instead of a compliant, docile public loyal to the employers who both fed it and sometimes poisoned it, an outraged and fearful nation watched with trepidation as each new story appeared.

Toxic sites soon surfaced across the country. The James River in Virginia was found to be loaded with a dangerous chemical called ketone. In Kentucky more than seventeen thousand corroding, leaking, oozing drums of hazardous waste had contaminated drinking water for populated areas. At Times Beach, Missouri, where dioxin, the name given to a class of supertoxic chemicals (the chlorinated dioxins and furans that are the by-product of the manufacture, molding, or burning of organic chemicals and plastics that contain chlorine), forced the abandonment of the town. Countless other places became symbols of the toxicity of progress. The nation had become prosperous, but at a price no one had imagined. In the early 1980s the price seemed to increase daily.

As public knowledge of contamination spread, one institution in American society continued to avoid scrutiny. The military was the leading polluter in the United States, yet its activities were almost entirely shielded from public view. With its enormous budget and its many and varied responsibilities, the armed forces maintained facilities not only across the country but in American territories and other countries around the world. With everything from weapons development to chemical and nuclear warfare in its purview, and throughout the cold war period from 1945 to 1989 able to use the claim of national security to deflect any inquiries, the military had learned a studied strategy of stonewalling when it came to toxic and hazardous waste management.

The Environmental Protection Agency had nominal jurisdiction over military activities that involved toxic and hazardous substances, but in the 1980s the agency was at its nadir. Its successes had begun after Love Canal and continued despite the election of Ronald Reagan, widely presumed to be anti-regulation and pro-business. The crowning legal achievement of the early EPA was the Comprehensive Environmental Response, Compensation and Liability Act of 1980 (CERCLA), known as the Superfund Act, which created a $1.6 billion fund for the cleanup of toxic waste sites and oil spills, financed by taxes on petroleum and other chemicals as well as federal appropriations. The agency seemed poised to regain some of the trust the federal government had lost during the 1970s, and if any agency could expose the military, the EPA seemed the best candidate.

But under Reagan, the EPA suffered. During the first year of the new administration, the agency lacked an administrator. A sharp decline in new enforcement cases, a resulting loss of credibility for the agency, and dwindling morale among career employees marked the first two years under Reagan. A procession of weak and controversial leaders hamstrung the EPA throughout the mid-eighties as Americans felt their faith in the agency betrayed. In a public outcry, even prominent Republicans challenged the actions of the Reagan administration. Russell A. Train, EPA administrator during the 1970s, sharply criticized the agency's leadership and direction in the *Washington Post*. Cartoonist Garry Trudeau savaged the agency in his comic strip, *Doonesbury*, implying that its leaders callously lied to the public on countless occasions.

The Reagan administration also worked to curtail the EPA's reach; the military especially benefited from this strategy. Enforcement standards were set so that the $1.6 billion Superfund would not be spent. This meant that the agency generally did not pursue law enforcement, instead resorting to sometimes fruitless negotiation with polluters. Without the willingness to litigate to compel violators to comply, the agency seemed weak and ineffectual. Later, in 1986, Reagan signed Executive Order 12580, which gave the Department of Justice the right to disapprove any EPA enforcement action against a federal facility. The Justice Department held that executive branch entities could not sue each other, effectively ending the EPA's ability to enforce its mandate on federal lands. The decision was a terrible blow to the EPA and to enforcement of the law.

Outraged, Congress responded by investigating. Congressman Mike Synar of Oklahoma opened a November 1987 meeting of the congressional Subcommittee on Environment, Energy, and Natural Resources with the observation that defense installations "should be held to the same strict standards of accountability" as civilian endeavors. Although the congressman had spent much of his career trying to hold the military accountable for the environmental damage it caused, even he was shocked at the vast number of instances of contamination and the remarkable disregard for the population that characterized much of military activity.

When Synar started to peel back the veil of secrecy, the numbers were astounding. The Pentagon recognized at least 4,611 contaminated sites at 761 military bases, some of which posed imminent threats to the public. At Lakehurst Naval Air Engineering Center in New Jersey, workers had dumped more than 3 million gallons of cancer-causing aviation fuel in an area that endangered the Cohansey Aquifer, the primary source of drinking water for most of southern New Jersey. The army's Cornhusker Ammunition Plant near Grand Island, Nebraska, had spilled so much explosive material that nearby drinking water wells were contaminated. Although by 1980 officials knew that both TNT and RDX leached beyond the installation's boundaries, the army chose not to notify people in the area. "We didn't want to get them overly anxious," a spokesman laconically remarked. McClellan Air Force Base in Sacramento, California, polluted at least 170 separate sites with routine dumping of toxic liquids, sludge, and solid wastes; leaks in underground storage tanks and waste lines; and accidental spills. The list of chemicals spilled included everything from contaminated oil to solvents. Even after pressure from the surrounding community, the air force cleaned up only one of the 170 sites and managed to study only 17 more.

Early in the 1990s the *Albuquerque Tribune*, the southwestern city's smaller afternoon paper, stumbled across a story of stunning social and political consequence. During the late 1940s and well into the 1950s, when scientists knew well the consequences of exposure to radioactive materials, the military had conducted experiments in which plutonium was injected into subjects who had no way to prevent the action. The mentally ill and the incarcerated were frequent choices. Initially the assumption was that the experiments, as these efforts were called, were confined to the Southwest, but it soon became known that similar instances had occurred around the country. Although not reaching the level of the Tuskegee syphilis experiments, in which this disease was not treated in poor African-American men so that physicians could confirm a well-known pattern of deterioration, the plutonium experiments were shocking examples of betrayal of faith by the government against the most defenseless of its citizens. If Americans needed another reason to mistrust their government on questions of toxicity, military science in the 1940s and 1950s surely provided it.

This dismal record buttressed the nation's anarchic individualist pose. In part the so-called Reagan Revolution encouraged this attitude; it was also a product of the growing displacement of industrial and white-collar workers left behind in the "downsizing" of business that swept the nation in the late 1980s and early 1990s. On the heels of the Sagebrush Rebellion, and as Americans' faith in their institutions plummeted, the question remained: could the sort of communitarian effort that had supported environmentalism sustain itself as the United States shifted to a postindustrial, service-based economy?

The answer to this question came in the many kinds of grass-roots environmental activism that emerged across the country in response to the lack of protection from conventional American mechanisms. From states such as Nevada, which faced a cavalier process that attempted to locate the nation's permanent high-level nuclear waste storage facility about a hundred miles from the largest city in the state, to local groups focused on specific issues in urban and rural locations, the effort to protect society from toxic dangers took shape. Committed and often single-minded attorneys grappled with corporations on behalf of a range of loosely connected organizations that accepted the premises of the quality-of-life movement. On the local scene, such alliances emerged as powerful players. As they had a century before, these groups and their members had overlapping interests, but they were rarely linked.

The ideas expressed by these groups were not always conventional environmentalism, but they surely embraced many of its tenets. Quality of life—in this case the right to be free of the deleterious effects of other people's actions—was clearly one of their more powerful concerns. So was their embrace of the need for balance between economic goals and the preservation of the natural world. From Love Canal to rural Oklahoma to the forests of northern California, people made their living off the land. They clearly recognized that disregard for it might reward them in the short term but damage their long-term future. They faced a difficult dilemma, especially as the decisions that affected their future came from farther and farther away. Their immediate needs and their children's futures collided, compelling difficult choices in hard situations. The result was pervasive tension in a range of situations.

The process of siting the first national high-level nuclear waste dump illustrated the ways that power in American society was distributed and how it could be turned to the advantage of the powerful. Nuclear reactors across the country produced radioactive waste, and by the early 1980s Congress determined that a permanent waste storage facility was essential. On December 13, 1980, it passed the Low-Level Nuclear Radioactive Waste Policy Act, designed to fashion a solution to the question of the disposal of low-level radioactive waste, the spent but still radioactive materials used in hospitals, universities, and laboratories. The passage of the Nuclear Waste Policy Act of 1982 (NWPAA) on December 20, 1982, tackled the far more difficult problem of high-level waste, the spent fuel rods and other radioactive materials that were left from the process of creating nuclear energy. This act directed the selection of five sites to be studied for the location of a permanent high-level waste storage facility. From the five, two would be selected—one east of the Mississippi River, one west. Science would dictate the choices: high-level nuclear waste could be located only in geological formations strong enough to withstand any disaster for more than ten thousand years, the amount of time required before the radioactive waste material ceased to be a threat to humanity.

But science was never a determinant in the decision-making process. Power and political will instead shaped the choices. In December 1984 the Department of Energy selected three sites as preferred choices to be examined for the first repository: Deaf Smith County in desolate west Texas; Yucca Mountain, northwest of Las Vegas, Nevada; and the Hanford Reservation in central Washington State. No locations in the East were included. They had been assigned to a second repository, much to the joy of the public east of the Mississippi. The three chosen sites seemed like good candidates for "national sacrifice zones." Hanford and Yucca Mountain, adjacent to the Nevada Test Site, had long histories of atomic and nuclear operations. The nearly vacant Deaf Smith County, Texas, was a few hours from the Pantex weapons plant at Amarillo. Officials supposed that people in all three places were unlikely to object strenuously to a repository.

But this was as far as the process went. Shortly after the initial selection, the Energy Department "indefinitely deferred" the search for a second site. Meanwhile, protests in Texas against the choice of Deaf Smith County and the vast power of the Texas congressional delegation made it hard to force the repository on a large and powerful state. Hanford was in a populated agricultural area along the Columbia River, and the Northwest had long been the home of strident environmentalism. That left Yucca Mountain, in the middle of a federal weapons range, in a state that was a colony of everywhere, a place that depended on other places for nearly everything it needed to survive. Combined with weak political representation, its fundamental nature made Nevada a target for a nuclear waste repository.

Yucca Mountain was marginally viable from a geological perspective, but from a political perspective it was ideal. In 1987 Senator Bennett Johnston, Democrat from Louisiana, and Senator James McClure, Republican from Idaho, introduced legislation to assess only Yucca Mountain, ending the search for any other location. Even if there had been safeguards, the record of the Energy Department and the huge sums necessary to "characterize" the site, to assure its adequacy as a repository, estimated at more than $1 billion in 1988, all but guaranteed that Yucca Mountain would be the location. With passage of the bill, the planned scientific process had become strictly political. Johnston's Yucca Mountain legislation became known as the "Screw Nevada" bill.

The bill became a galvanizing factor in Nevada, a way for residents of the most libertarian state in the Union to see the heavy hand of the federal government upon them once again. The Nevada legislature opposed NWPAA and the Yucca Mountain project with the passage of Assembly Bill 222 in 1989, which made it illegal to dispose of high-level nuclear waste in Nevada. Despite widespread efforts to purchase the goodwill of the Nevada public—in one instance a well-known television news correspondent put his hard-won credibility at the service of the Energy Department and Yucca Mountain for a considerable fee, declaring his support for the dump— and the creation of the Yucca Mountain Science Center in Las Vegas to "educate" the public, Nevadans saw this breach of states' rights as a threat to the state's integrity. They opposed the site and effectively boycotted the Yucca Mountain Science Center. "The only people who visit," a high-level official remarked, "are family and friends," testimony to both the resentment of federal authority in Nevada and the widespread fear of nuclear waste in a state that produced none of its own but had long been the national testing ground for atomic weapons.

Systematic resistance to the nuclear waste dump in Nevada was the most well-heeled and organized grassroots resistance in the nation. But there were many others. Lois Gibbs, who organized the Love Canal Homeowners Association, went on to found the Citizens' Clearinghouse for Hazardous Waste and become its executive director. Attorneys such as Jan Schlichtmann, who sued W. R. Grace and Beatrice Foods on behalf of the people of Woburn, Massachusetts, in the case that became the basis for the book *A Civil Action*, exemplified the new breed of grassroots activists. Unlike the environmental rebels of the 1960s, these people were part of communities, believed in government and its power to redress wrongs, and were often intimately dependent on the very industries they protested. What they sought was not an end to human activities in the physical world—a trait often attributed to radical environmental groups—but responsible behavior in the natural world to allow people the full benefits of their lives and to ensure a future for their children. This philosophy resembled nothing so much as Gifford Pinchot's famed conservation ethos: "The greatest good for the greatest number in the long run."

This search for balance best explains why the groups that have challenged environmental goals in the United States have not generally succeeded. Americans are fundamentally centrists, products of a nation with enough wealth and opportunity to assure a wide middle. Extreme positions, be it Earth First! with its doctrine of "No compromise in defense of Mother Nature," or the Wise Use movement, which advocates development at nature's expense, tempts many but rarely carries the day. Even the vast corporate funding that frequently supports the opponents of environmentalism has failed to persuade most Americans. Many remember a time when a lack of regulation meant polluted skies and fouled water. Still more mistrust government, especially when it comes to taking care of their health, and even more believe in the rhetoric of democracy, the idea that people of goodwill but differing perspectives need not erase one another from the face of the earth in order to achieve acceptable goals.

This was the first lesson the 104th Congress learned upon taking office in early 1995. Seen as the backlash Congress, this first Congress in which Republicans comprised a majority in both houses since the 1950s swept into power on a platform that promised to dismantle government interference in everyday life. Its famed Contract with America was supposed to help ordinary people, but within months the Republican leadership found that while they had the support of the public in an abstract sense, Americans valued the protection of their environment in surprising ways. Free from pollution and most of the hazards of toxicity for more than a generation, and possessed of a mechanism for the cleanup of hazardous waste in the Superfund, Americans expected to retain those protections in law. The 104th Congress may have anticipated a nation with only a few rules, but the public had not. The losses that Republicans experienced in the 1996 and 1998 elections illustrated the degree to which Americans were committed to the consensus of balance that professional environmentalism had come to contain.

In essence, conservation and environmentalism had come full circle in the twentieth century. Americans had begun the century with a fear of scarcity, but in prosperous times they showed a willingness to set aside resources in perpetuity. In harder economic times they shifted away from an all-or-nothing ethos back toward a more commonsensical center, where people used the environment but sought to protect themselves from both the results of rapacious use—activities such as clear-cutting, strip mining, or cyanide-induced gold mining, which took the tops off of mountains—and the consequences of the processes they depended upon. As a freshman in Congress, Oklahoma Representative Mike Synar was warned against taking on a Superfund project in his district because Oklahomans were not environmentalists. Synar agreed: Oklahomans "aren't environmentalists. They're conservationists," he told David Helvarg, author of *The War Against the Greens.* "The ranching community believes in their heart that they had to leave [the land] better than they found it. The hunters like to have adequate game and good fishing for fishermen. . . . So when you start dirtying their water and filthying their air and cutting them off" from the pursuits they enjoy, "they're [still] not environmentalists but you have changed their ability to enjoy their life and they'll be first in line to take a stand."

In the end this combination of NIMBY—"Not in My Backyard"—and quality of life held more power for Americans than any ideal of environmentalism. As environmentalists, Americans were pale green; they embraced the theory as long as the practice did not cause them personal pain. As people who maximized their self-interest in an enlightened fashion, who saw quality of life as a right and not a privilege, who valued their relationship to place above much else, and who believed that the center held more for everybody than any extreme, Americans served as stewards in a sense that progressive conservationists would have understood. Finally, they stood for a balance—between making a living and protecting nature, between the rights of the individual and the goals of community. Despite political turmoil in the nation as the century ended, Americans remained committed to a set of ideas that the people at the beginning of the twentieth century would have understood and respected. They feared loss and embraced a view of the long term designed to prevent it. In this way they faced the twenty-first century as they their forebears had its predecessors, with fear and optimism, with enthusiasm for challenges and an eye for the way changes would affect them.

A Note on Sources

CONSERVATION and environmentalism have become among the most widely investigated subjects in American historical writing. Among the best general efforts are Samuel P. Hays, *Conservation and the Gospel of Efficiency: The Progressive Conservation Movement, 1880–1920* (Cambridge, Mass., 1959), and *Beauty, Health, and Permanence: Environmental Politics in the United States, 1955–1985* (Cambridge, England, 1987); Robert Gottlieb, *Forcing the Spring: The Transformation of the American Environmental Movement* (Washington, D.C., 1993); Riley Dunlap and Angela Mertig, eds., *American Environmentalism: The U.S. Environmental Movement, 1970–1990* (Bristol, Pa., 1992); Raymond F. Dasmann, *The Destruction of California* (New York, 1965); Walter A. Rosenbaum, *The Politics of Environmental Concern* (Westport, Conn., 1973); Clive Ponting, *A Green History of the World* (London, 1991); Victor B. Sheffer, *The Shaping of Environmentalism in America* (Seattle, 1991); and Roderick Nash, *Wilderness and the American Mind* (New Haven, Conn., 1982) 3rd edition. Bryan Norton, *Toward Unity Among Environmentalists* (New York, 1991) presents a new point of view, while Max Oelschlager, *The Idea of Wilderness: From Prehistory to the Age of Ecology* (New Haven, Conn., 1991), amply surveys the intellectual idea of wilderness.

The best works on turn-of-the-century conservation are Michael P. Cohen, *The History of the Sierra Club, 1892–1970* (Santa Fe, N.Mex., 1988), a masterful history of the organization; and Stephen Fox, *John Muir and His Legacy: The American Conservation Movement* (Boston, 1981), which tracks the legacy of Muir's impulse through the century. Martin V. Melosi, *Pollution and Reform in American Cities, 1870–1930* (Austin, Tex., 1980), and Joel Tarr, *The Search for the Ultimate Sink: Urban Pollution in*

Historical Perspective (Akron, Ohio, 1996) offer the best views of the relationship between pollution, technology, and reform as the twentieth century began.

Water has its own bibliography. Marc Reisner, *Cadillac Desert: The American West and Its Disappearing Water* (New York, 1986); Norris Hundley, Jr., *The Great Thirst: Californians and Water, 1770s–1990s* (Berkeley, 1992); Donald Worster, *Rivers of Empire: Water, Aridity, and the Growth of the American West* (New York, 1985); and Donald J. Pisani, *From Family Farm to Agribusiness: The Irrigation Crusade in California and the West, 1850–1931* (Berkeley, 1984) have defined the turf. Although these authors often disagree, together they provide a comprehensive look at the politics of the distribution of water.

Federal agencies have been the subject of a great deal of historical writing. David A. Clary, *Timber and the Forest Service* (Lawrence, Kans., 1986), and Paul Hirt, *A Conspiracy of Optimism: Management of the National Forests Since World War Two* (Lincoln, Nebr., 1994) together comprise a powerful critique of that agency; Harold K. Steen, *The United States Forest Service: A History* (Seattle, 1976) offers a less critical view. For the National Park Service, see Alfred Runte, *National Parks: The American Experience* (Lincoln, Nebr., 1987), 2nd edition; Hal K. Rothman, *America's National Monuments: The Politics of Preservation* (Lawrence, Kans., 1994); John Freemuth, *Islands Under Siege: National Parks and the Politics of External Threats* (Lawrence, Kans., 1991); and Richard W. Sellars, *Preserving Nature in the National Parks: A History* (New Haven, Conn., 1997). Reisner's and Worster's works on water, cited above, cover the Bureau of Reclamation, while the history of the Corps of Engineers has not yet been the subject of a comprehensive scholarly book. The best is the Corps' own *History of the US Army Corps of Engineers* (Washington, D.C., 1998), 2nd edition.

The transformation of conservation into environmentalism is closely connected to the Echo Park controversy. Mark W. T. Harvey, *A Symbol of Wilderness: Echo Park and the American Conservation Movement* (Albuquerque, N.Mex., 1994) is the standard work. David R. Brower, ed., *The Place No One Knew: Glen*

Canyon on the Colorado (Santa Fe, N.Mex., 1968), expresses this leader's regret over the sacrifice of Glen Canyon.

Novels, memoirs, and popular nonfiction have been highly influential in the environmental movement. Among the most intriguing are Terry Tempest Williams, *Refuge: An Unnatural History of Family and Place* (New York, 1991); Edward Abbey, *The Monkey Wrench Gang* (Salt Lake City, 1985), reprint; Rachel Carson, *Silent Spring* (New York, 1962); Dave Foreman, *Confessions of an Eco-Warrior* (New York, 1991); Stewart Udall, *The Quiet Crisis* (New York, 1963); and John McPhee, *Encounters with the Archdruid* (New York, 1970), all of whom helped shape the debate about the environment, but in very different ways. Abbey incited, leading to ecologically based movements such as Earth First!; Terry Tempest Williams explained in heartfelt terms the odyssey of the downwinders, and Dave Foreman explained advocacy and his own personal evolution. Carson, Udall, and McPhee illustrated in high relief the issues of their time, offering a literary statement as well as check on the values of their society.

Questions of urban toxicity have until recently been the province of journalists. Michael Brown, *Laying Waste: The Poisoning of America by Toxic Chemicals* (New York, 1979), stands out for its focus and clarity. Michael D'Antonio, *Atomic Harvest: Hanford and the Lethal Toll of America's Nuclear Arsenal* (New York, 1993) offers a look into the practices of the military. Scholars have begun to address these topics as well. Craig E. Colten and Peter F. Skinner, *The Road to Love Canal: Managing Industrial Waste Before EPA* (Austin, Tex., 1996) offer an insightful history of water management. James Whorton, *Before Silent Spring: Pesticides and Public Health in Pre-DDT America* (Princeton, 1974), and Thomas R. Dunlap, *DDT: Scientists, Citizens, and Public Policy* (Princeton, 1981) set the debate over DDT in context. Joel B. Goldsteen, *Danger All Around: Waste Storage Crisis on the Texas and Louisiana Gulf Coast* (Austin, Tex., 1993) shows the consequences of unbridled industrial development. Kenneth T. Jackson, *Crabgrass Frontier: The Suburbanization of the United States* (New York, 1985), a classic work, helps describe the culture of postwar society and opens the way to understanding the context of environmentalism.

Environmental justice has attracted a great deal of recent attention. Robert Bullard, *Dumping in Dixie: Race, Class, and Environmental Quality* (Boulder, Colo., 1990) is credited with initiating the scholarly debate. David Schlosberg, *Environmental Justice and the New Pluralism: The Challenge of Difference for Environmentalism* (New York, 1999) offers a complicated challenge to the conventional wisdom. Andrew Hurley, *Environmental Inequalities: Class, Race, and Industrial Pollution in Gary, Indiana, 1945–1980* (Chapel Hill, 1995) offers the first comprehensive case study of an environmental justice setting; Laura Pulido, *Environmentalism and Economic Justice: Two Chicano Struggles in the Southwest* (Tucson, 1996) adds Hispanics to a mix often framed in black and white.

On the Wise Use and property rights movements, R. McGreggor Cawley, *Federal Land, Western Anger: The Sagebrush Rebellion and Environmental Politics* (Lawrence, Kans., 1993) is the most general look at the issues. William L. Graf, *Wilderness Preservation and the Sagebrush Rebellions* (Lanham, Md., 1990) ties these two issues closely together. Phillip Brick and R. McGreggor Cawley, eds., *The Land Rights Movement and Renewing American Environmentalism* (Lanham, Md., 1996) present a survey of the question. Clearly more remains to be written about this phenomenon.

Much in fact remains to be written about environmentalism as a whole. Its rapid emergence in American society and the transition from advocacy to analysis among scholars mean that plenty of avenues remain for those interested in pursuing these topics.

Index

Abbey, Edward, 172–173
Acadia National Park, 64
Addams, Jane, 16
African Americans, 88, 162, 198
Albright, Horace M., 63, 64, 66
American Forestry Association, 72
American Museum of Natural
    History, 27, 73
Anderson, Clinton P., 105, 168
Antiquities Act of 1906, 48, 51–52, 54,
    56, 177
Arnold, Ron, 177–179
Aspinall, Wayne, 149, 168
Atomic Energy Act of 1954, 152
Atomic Energy Commission, 151,
    154, 185
Atomic testing, 115, 116, 117,
    151–152, 155, 185
"Atoms for Peace," 151
Audubon Association, 73, 170–171

Ballinger, Richard A., 47
Ballinger-Pinchot controversy, 46
Bandelier National Monument, 149
Bechtel, 98
Bell, Daniel, 94
Bell, Thomas, 91
Benson, Ezra Taft, 119
Berg, Alan, 176
Bible, Alan, 168
Bikini Islands, 115, 116, 152
Bonneville Dam, 77
Boone and Crockett Club, 29–30
Boulder Dam, 67, 70, 72, 98, 99
Bradley, David, 116, 152
Brower, David, 96, 97, 102, 103,
    106

Brown and Root, 98
Bryan, William Jennings, 32
Bryce Canyon National Park, 63
Buffon, Comte Georges de, 18
Bulletin, 96
Burford, Anne Gorsuch, 175
Burford, Robert, 175
Burroughs, John, 18
Burton, Phillip, 168
Butler, Ovid M., 73

Canyon de Chelly National
    Monument, 27
Carey Act of 1894, 49
Carlsbad, New Mexico, 116
Carnegie, Andrew, 16
Carson, Rachel, 8, 113, 117, 118, 120,
    150, 189
Carter, Jimmy, 154, 159, 161, 194
Carver, Richard, 180–182
Casa Grande National Monument,
    28
Center for the Defense of Free
    Enterprise (CDFE), 178
Chaco Culture National Historic
    Park, 27
Chaffey, George, 67, 68
Chapman, Oscar, 102
Chernobyl, 189
China Syndrome, 187, 189
Cholera, 40–42
Church Rock, New Mexico, 189
Civilian Conservation Corps (CCC),
    74, 75
Cleveland, Grover, 32
Cody, Iron Eyes, 113, 129
Cody, William F., 49

Coldiron, William, 169
Colorado River, 67, 68, 69, 103
Colorado River Compact, 69
Colorado River Storage Project (CRSP), 86, 99, 101, 105, 106
Columbia River, 77
Comprehensive Environmental Response, Compensation and Liability Act of 1980 (CERCLA), 196
Coolidge, Calvin, 65, 66
Cooper, James Fenimore, 18, 29
Council of Conservationists, 106
Council on Environmental Quality, 138
County Movement, 180–182
Cross-Florida Barge Canal, 140
"Culture and custom," 163
Curry Company, 96

Denton, Winfield S., 168
Devil's Postpile National Monument, 56
DeVoto, Bernard, 135–136
Diablo Canyon, 185
Dichloro-diphenyl-trichloroethane (DDT), 118, 189–190
Dinosaur National Monument, 8, 86, 87, 99, 101, 102, 103, 106, 107
Doheny, Edward F., 65
Dominy, Floyd, 99, 100
Dos Passos, John, 12, 62
Dreiser, Theodore, 38
Drury, Newton, 102, 103
Dust Bowl, 79, 80, 81

Earth Day, 146–147, 156
Earth First!, 171–173, 203
Easy Rider, 111
Echo Park Dam, 8, 87, 99, 101–107, 135, 159, 167–168
Eisenhower, Dwight D., 151
Emergency Conservation Work program, 75
Emerson, Ralph Waldo, 5

Endangered Species Conservation Act of 1973, 134, 159–162, 177
Environmental Action, 147
Environmental impact statement (EIS), 138–144, 147
Environmental Protection Agency, 140–141, 192–194, 196–197
Erlich, Paul, 113, 120, 121, 124
Etnier, David, 161
Executive Order 12580, 197

Fall, Albert B., 65, 66
Federal Land Policy and Management Act, 165
Federal Radiation Council, 140
Federal Water Quality Administration, 140
Fermi, Enrico, 82
Flood Control Act of 1936, 77
Fonda, Jane, 187
Food and Drug Administration (FDA), 118, 119
Ford, Gerald, 158
Foreman, Dave, 171–174
Forest Reserve Act of 1897, 26
Friedan, Betty, 94
Friends of the Earth, 173

General Appropriations Act of 1891, 25–26, 28
General Motors Corporation, 92
George, Henry, 13
Gilded Age, 22, 42
Glacier National Park, 101
Glacier View Dam, 101
Glen Canyon Dam, 87, 132, 172
Goldwater, Barry, 163, 178
Gottlieb, Alan, 177–178
Grand Canyon National Park, 33, 53, 54, 63, 85
Grand Teton National Park, 63
Great Plains, 77, 78, 79
Great Smoky Mountains National Park, 64
Green Revolution, 121

Greenpeace, 171
Grinnell, George Bird, 30, 31, 32

Hanford Reservation, 155
Hardin, Garrett, 122, 123, 124, 128
Harding, Warren G., 65, 66
Harriman, Edward H., 68
Harrison, Benjamin, 26, 35
Hatch, Orrin, 164
Heritage Foundation, 177
Hetch-Hetchy, 55–58, 87
Hickel, Walter J., 142–143
"High Trip," 23–24, 97
Homestead Act of 1862, 12, 26
Hooker Chemical Company,
    191–194
Hoover, Herbert, 66
Hoover Dam, 67, 99
House Public Lands Committee, 31
Hudson River School, 18
Humphrey, Hubert, 135
"Hydrocarbon Man," 94

Ickes, Harold L., 74, 83, 98
Imperial Valley, 67, 68, 70
Interstate Commerce Act of 1887, 16,
    17
Izaak Walton League, 85, 95

Jackson, Leroy, 179
James River, Virginia, 195
Jefferson, Thomas, 12
Johnson, "Lady Bird," 125–126, 129
Johnson, Lyndon B., 78, 105, 113, 137
Johnson, Robert Underwood, 21, 22
Johnston, Bennett, 201
Jordan, David Starr, 21

Kamen, Martin D., 154
Kennedy, John F., 113, 120, 137
Kent, William, 56
Keynes, John Maynard, 72
King, Martin Luther, Jr., 115, 130
Koehler, Bart, 173
Krug, Julius, 100, 102

Lacey, John F., 31
Lacey Act of 1894, 31
Lacey Act of 1900, 31
Land Management, Bureau of, 136,
    149, 163–166
LAS detergents, 127
Las Vegas, 116, 180, 201–202
League for the Advancement of
    States' Equal Rights, 166
LeConte, Joseph, 21
Leopold, Aldo, 97, 137
Levittown, 89
Lewis and Clark, 14
Livermore, Norman, 95
Los Angeles, 58, 66, 68, 82, 93
Louisiana Purchase, 14
Love Canal, 191–195, 199, 202
Low-Level Nuclear Radioactive
    Waste Policy Act of 1980, 200
Lucky Dragon, 152
Lummis, Charles F., 18

Malthus, Thomas, 120
Mammoth Cave National Park, 64
Manifest Destiny, 14
Marsh, George Perkins, 5
Marshall, Robert, 137
Martin, Joseph W., Jr., 105
Mather, Stephen T., 63, 64, 66
Maxwell, George H., 49
McClure, James, 201
McKay, Douglas, 100, 105
McKinley, William, 32, 34
Mead, Elwood, 66
Mesa Verde National Park, 27
Microchip Revolution, 182
Millikin, Eugene, 105
Mission 66, 136
Mondale, Walter, 176
Monkey Wrench Gang (Abbey), 172
Monongahela River, 91
Montana Power Company, 169
Moran, Thomas, 18
Morgan, Susan, 173
Morrill Land Grant Act, 12

Morrison-Knudsen, 98
Morton, C. B. Rogers, 144
Mount Olympus National
    Monument, 53
Muir, John, 19, 20, 21, 22, 23, 24, 33,
    37, 56–58, 64, 83, 111
Murie, Olaus, 101
Muscle Shoals, 75
Muskie, Edmund, 138

National Air Pollution Control
    Administration, 140
National Association of
    Manufacturers, 49
National Board of Trade, 49
National Business Men's League, 49
National Environmental Policy Act
    of 1969 (NEPA), 138–144, 147
National Irrigation Congress, 49
National Park Service, 63, 64, 65, 101,
    102, 105, 136, 149, 178
National Parks and Conservation
    Association, 171–173
National Parks Association, 73
National Rifle Association, 177
National Wildlife Federation, 95, 171
Native Americans, 17, 27, 29, 66, 113,
    129, 179
Natural Resources Defense Council,
    171
Nelson, Gaylord, 138
Nevada Test Site, 154, 181, 184
New Deal, 61, 62, 72, 74, 77, 80, 81
Newlands, Francis G., 49, 50, 56
Nixon, Richard M., 138, 139, 149
No Place to Hide (Bradley), 116, 152
North Coast Water Company, 56
Northern Securities Company, 36–37
"Not in My Backyard" (NIMBY),
    156, 205
Nuclear power, 152–154
Nuclear Regulatory Commission, 154
Nuclear Waste Policy Act of 1982,
    200–202
Nye County, Nevada, 180–182

Oak Ridge National Laboratory, 155
Olney, Warren, 21, 23
O'Mahoney, Joseph, 105
Operation Crossroads, 115
Oppenheimer, J. Robert, 114, 154
Organization of Petroleum
    Exporting Countries (OPEC), 145,
    158, 169
Owens Valley, 58, 66, 68

Page, Arizona, 149, 153
Pan-American Company, 65
Pan-American Exposition, 34
Panama Canal, 71
Peabody Coal Company, 149
Peabody Museum, 27
Pence, Guy, 181
Petrified Forest National Monument,
    51
Pickens, Homer, 129
Pinchot, Gifford, 5, 33, 37, 42, 43, 44,
    45, 46, 47, 57, 75, 83, 203
Pittsburgh, Pennsylvania, 40–42
Place That No One Knew (Porter),
    87
Polychlorinated biphenyls (PCBs),
    191
Population Bomb (Erlich), 113, 120,
    121
Porter, Elliot, 87
Powell, John Wesley, 26, 27, 48, 51
Pratt, George Dupont, 73
Price-Anderson Amendment, 152
Progressivism, 37–40, 41, 44, 47, 48,
    51, 54–55, 58, 62, 72, 98, 103, 135
Project Gasbuggy, 152
Project Rulison, 152
Public Works Administration, 75
Pure Food and Drug Act of 1906, 37,
    55

"Quality of life," 4, 7, 109, 110, 117,
    130, 137–138, 145–146, 149–150,
    153, 156, 162, 170, 199, 205
Quiet Crisis (Udall), 113, 114

Reagan, Ronald, 95, 140, 163–170, 174–176, 199
Reclamation Act of 1902, 48, 51, 104, 105
Reclamation, Bureau of, 51, 66, 70, 77, 87, 98, 99, 149
Redwood National Park, 174
Reed, Nathaniel P., 169
Reisner, Marc, 99
Riesman, David, 94
Riis, Jacob, 16
Roadless Area Review and Evaluation (RARE), 150
Robinson, Charles D., 23
Rockefeller, John D., 11
Rockwood, Charles, 67, 68
Rocky Flats Nuclear Arsenal, 152, 155, 188
Roosevelt, Franklin D., 61, 72, 73, 74, 98
Roosevelt, Theodore, 14, 30–31, 33–38, 42, 44, 45, 47, 51–53, 71, 86
Roselle, Mike, 173
Ruckelshaus, William, 169

Sagebrush Rebellion, 162–168, 173, 175, 199
Sagebrush rebels, 164
Salt River Project, 51
San Joaquin Water Company, 56
Sand County Almanac (Leopold), 97
Santa Barbara, California, 127–128, 134, 138, 167
Saylor, John, 135
Second Amendment Foundation, 178
Shenandoah National Park, 64
Sherman Anti-Trust Act of 1890, 16, 17
Sieberling, John, 168
Sierra Club, 20–21, 22, 23, 24, 56, 95, 96, 97, 101, 104, 106, 145, 170–171, 173, 178, 184
Silent Spring (Carson), 8, 113, 119, 120, 150, 189

Sinclair, Harry F., 65
Skubitz, Joe, 168
"Smog," 93
Smokey Bear, 129, 130
Smythe, William E., 49
Social Darwinism, 13
Soil Conservation Service, 80, 81
Spencer, Herbert, 13
Standard Oil, 11
Stegner, Wallace, 103, 113
Steinbeck, John, 80
Stewart, Alice, 152
Stoneman Meadows, 122
Straus, Mike, 99
Superfund, 197, 204
Swing-Johnson Bill, 69
Synar, Mike, 197, 204

Taos Commune, 124
Teapot Dome Scandal, 65
Teller, Edward, 154
Tellico Dam project, 161–162
Tennessee Valley Authority, 61, 74, 75, 76, 77
Thoreau, Henry David, 5
Three Mile Island, 187–189
Timber and Stone Act of 1878, 26
Timber Culture Act of 1873, 26
Times Beach, Missouri, 195
Train, Russell, 169, 196
Trans-Alaska Pipeline System (TAPS), 142–143
Trinity Site, 83
Tuolomne Meadows, 22
Turner, Frederick Jackson, 14, 44, 114

Udall, Stewart, 113, 114, 115, 119
Union of Concerned Scientists, 185
United Nations Scientific Committee on the Effects of Radiation (UNSCEAR), 152
University of Chicago, 82
U.S. Army Corps of Engineers, 70, 71, 72, 75, 98, 101, 140

U.S. Forest Service, 45, 46, 65, 130, 136, 150, 172, 180
U.S. Steel, 92
Utah Power and Light, 153

Vanderbilt, Cornelius, 16
Vanderbilt, George W., 44

Wagner Electric Company, 191
Walsh, Thomas J., 65
Ward, Lester Frank, 13
Washington, Booker T., 35
Watergate, 159
Watkins, Arthur, 105
Watt, James, 166–173, 175–176
Weathermen, 112
Whyte, William H., 94
Wilbur, Ray Lyman, 66
Wild Horse and Burro Act of 1971, 134
Wilderness Act of 1964, 134, 137
Wilderness Society, 85, 95, 97, 98, 101, 102, 135, 170, 172
Wilson, Woodrow, 45

Winchell, Walter, 92
Wirth, Connie, 102, 105
Wise Use movement, 177–180, 181, 203
Wolke, Howie, 173
Wood, Grant, 62
Works Progress Administration, 75
World War I, 63
World War II, 3, 4, 6, 8, 61, 81, 85, 87–89, 92, 97, 99, 101, 109–110, 114, 126, 129, 132, 151, 155
Worster, Donald, 99
Wyoming v. California, 69, 70

Yellowstone National Park, 30, 31, 33
Yergin, Daniel, 94
Yosemite National Park, 19, 20, 24, 55–58, 96, 167
Yucca Mountain, 181, 201–202

Zahniser, Howard, 98, 102, 103, 135, 136, 137, 160
Zion National Park, 63

A NOTE ON THE AUTHOR

Hal K. Rothman is the editor of *Environmental History* and is professor of history at the University of Nevada, Las Vegas. Born in Baton Rouge, Louisiana, he studied at the University of Texas. His other books include *Devil's Bargains: Tourism in the Twentieth-Century American West*, which received the Western Writers of America Spur Award for contemporary nonfiction; *The Greening of the Nation?: Environmentalism in the U.S. Since 1945*; *"I'll Never Fight Fire with My Bare Hands Again": Recollections of the First Forest Rangers of the Inland Northwest*; *On Rims and Ridges: The Los Alamos Area Since 1880*; and *Preserving Different Pasts: The American National Monuments*.